T0171470

THE ULTIMATE GUIDE:

Making Your Relationship Last

Tantric Lovers

HANNA KATZ-JELFS

BALBOA
PRESS

A DIVISION OF HAY HOUSE

TANTRIC LOVERS
Copyright © 2012 Hanna Katz-Jelfs.

All rights reserved. No part of this book may be used or reproduced by any means,
graphic, electronic, or mechanical, including photocopying, recording, taping or by any
information storage retrieval system without the written permission of the publisher
except in the case of brief quotations embodied in critical articles and reviews.

Balboa Press books may be ordered through booksellers or by contacting:

Balboa Press
A Division of Hay House
1663 Liberty Drive
Bloomington, IN 47403
www.balboapress.com
1-(877) 407-4847

Graphics/art submitted for the book by KFS from www.kerryfleur.com/

Because of the dynamic nature of the Internet, any web addresses or links contained in
this book may have changed since publication and may no longer be valid. The views
expressed in this work are solely those of the author and do not necessarily reflect the
views of the publisher, and the publisher hereby disclaims any responsibility for them.

The author of this book does not dispense medical advice or prescribe the use of any
technique as a form of treatment for physical, emotional, or medical problems without the
advice of a physician, either directly or indirectly. The intent of the author is only to offer
information of a general nature to help you in your quest for emotional and spiritual well-
being. In the event you use any of the information in this book for yourself, which is your
constitutional right, the author and the publisher assume no responsibility for your actions.

Printed in the United States of America

ISBN: 978-1-4525-6567-5 (sc)
ISBN: 978-1-4525-6569-9 (hc)
ISBN: 978-1-4525-6568-2(e)

Library of Congress Control Number: 2012923857

Balboa Press rev. date: 12/21/2012

Invocation Mantra

Aum Gam Gana Patayei Namaha

The Ganesh Mantra is dedicated to the success of our journey. Ganesh is a Hindu deity with a human body and an elephant head. He represents the energy that removes obstacles. Traditionally, this mantra is to be chanted 108 times.

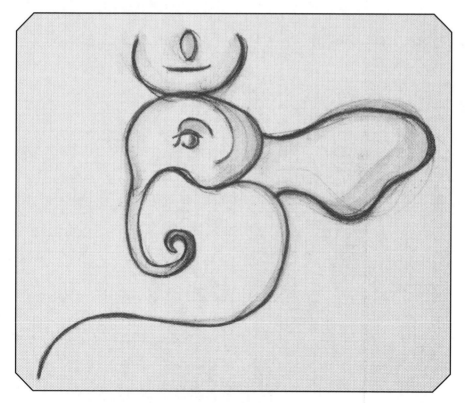

Image 03: Ganesh Aum

To all of us, all humanity. Let us share, honour, benefit from and celebrate our differences.

Let us rejoice in our diversity, honouring the divine in each and every one of us.

To world peace, to bringing enlightenment, to feeding our souls with the food of love.

To claiming our sexuality and liberating our true sensual nature in a spiritual honouring.

To my loved ones and future generations.

Namaste (I salute the divinity within you).

SANSKRIT BLESSING

Sarve Bhavantu Sukhinah. (May all be happy.)

Sarve Santu Niraamaya. (May all be free from dis-ease.)

Sarve Bhadraani Pashyantu. (May all sentient beings have well-being.)

Maa Kaschiduh Khabhaag Bhavait. (May none be in misery or suffering.)

Aum Shanti, Shanti, Shanti Aum. (Aum, I am peace, I am serenity, I am tranquility, Aum.)

FOREWORD

IT IS WITHOUT QUESTION that almost everything that has an impact on life has its foundation in relationships – good relationships, bad relationships, business relationships, family relationships, and most important of all, intimate relationships.

Without due consideration and care, each one of those relationships will wither and die, leaving a chasm only to be filled with loss, anger, and regret. Enriching life and living means engaging with it wholeheartedly, and that takes skills and training. It is with that approach that Hanna opens up her most successful secrets, and it is undoubtedly the way to a happier and more fulfilling life.

I have known Hanna for over seven years and have worked closely with her. She understands the human spirit and has guided many people on to a better and more stable path of intimacy. Her clients become fans, and her fans become friends. This book will open the way to those who have yet to experience the total and wholehearted commitment that she brings, and it will give just a peek through the crack in the door at a life more fulfilled and more enriched than they ever thought possible.

Don't take my word for it. Read and enjoy this book with an open mind, and most of all, enjoy being human. It can only last a lifetime, so why not?

Paul Haley, MBA, Business Strategy
at University of Southampton
paul@sterlingbusiness.co.uk
www.unfairadvantage.org.uk

PREFACE

THE OUTPOURING OF LOVE that is generated between lovers is the medicine of our time. As the wisdom of all ages collides with a modern world in the middle of a massive breakdown, those on a spiritual journey know that breakdowns lead to breakthroughs and the awakening of the heart. Sacred sexual union offers a way for men and women to restore connection to the infinite within themselves, and in relationship to others, as we all begin the great work of restoring and renewing our world.

Hanna Katz-Jelf's book *The Ultimate Guide for Tantric Lovers* offers a 'next step' on that journey of awakening by extending your personal awakening into the understanding of intimate relationship as a spiritual practice. This book unlocks the ancient secrets of arousing and sustaining sexual ecstasy by showing you how to activate and embody the pleasure of your own true spiritual nature.

This *Ultimate Guide* has simplified a variety of complex esoteric philosophies and spiritual practices from Hindu-yogic tantric texts, Tibetan Vajrayana Buddhist Tantric wisdom traditions, Taoist tantric understandings, and sacred teachings from the ancient Hebrew Tree of Life, along with contemporary scientific understanding of sensation, perception, and the brain's neurophysiology, to give you answers to hard questions ranging from 'What happens, and why does tantra work?' to 'Where I do begin?'

This is a good book to read on your own or with your partner, to learn how to regenerate yourself, deepen the love in your intimate relationships, expand trust in life, and cultivate faith in the process.

Exercises range from couples' practices to solo sex and more. You will find illuminating teachings on subtle anatomy and pleasure points, along with lesser-known erotic zones, all designed to help you to find the still point of Divine Presence amidst the rising waves and life's ecstatic crescendos of love's spiritual fires. It is an antidote to the loneliness, fear, desperation, and grief that riddle our lives with guilt, shame, depression, and anxiety. The best things in life truly are free, and tantra provides one of the 'true' paths to liberation from a world spinning out of control in the throes of accelerated change – all the symptoms of our current day and age, called the *Kali Yuga* by the ancient Hindu Vishnu Purana texts. Tantra is the spiritual practice of choice during the *Kali Yuga*.

This is one of the best books on tantra that I have seen in years. It unlocks the ancient secrets of awakening and sustaining sexual ecstasy by embodying the pleasure of our spiritual nature, including everything from anatomy to pleasure points and practices for couples, solo sex and more.

Dr Beth Hedva, PhD

(Dr Hedva is Director of Training and Counselling, Canadian Institute for Transpersonal and Integrative Sciences, and the author of the awarding-winning *Betrayal, Trust and Forgiveness*. She has an MA in clinical psychology, M.A. Her certifications and experience include: Transpersonal Counselling Psychology Registered Psychologist, Alberta #3212; NWT 2250 Marriage & Family Therapist, AAMFT #69225; Canadian Registry Marriage, Family and Child Counsellor, CA, BBSE# MFT MA18470; Director of Training and Counselling, Finkleman Communications LTD; co-founder, Canadian Institute for Transpersonal and Integrative Sciences; adjunct research faculty, Global Program, Sofia University (formerly Institute of Transpersonal Psych.); past chair of Continuing Education, International Council of Psychologists. More information is available at http://www.hedva. com, http://www.drbethhedva.com, and http://www.facebook.com/ beth.hedvaphd. Tel: 403.247.1441.)

ALSO BY THE SAME AUTHOR

A two-DVD set, *The Ultimate Guide to Tantric Healing Massage for Lovers*. First published June 2011, produced by Hanna Katz-Jelfs

Tantra is the mother, yoga is the son.

—Swami Satyananada Saraswati,
founder of the Bihar School of Yoga

Energy is the only life and is from the body ... energy is eternal delight.

—William Blake from *The Marriage of Heaven and Hell*

Tantra is embodied spirituality, awakening to aliveness to realize Oneness.

—Martin Jelfs, Transcendence www.tantra.uk.com

Tantra is the yoga of relationships and the art of honouring sacred sexuality.

—Hanna Katz-Jelfs, Maha Shakti Kali Ma,
Transcendence www.tantra.uk.com

TABLE OF CONTENTS

LIST OF ILLUSTRATIONS AND CHARTS

ACKNOWLEDGEMENTS

GRATITUDE AND THANKS TO you for being open-minded and receptive, for learning how to heal and celebrate our precious lives. Thanks for being respectful of this work and for purchasing this book. I wish you all that you desire.

To my beloved husband, Martin Jelfs, for the time, space, and freedom to develop this book and the DVDs, for supporting me throughout, and for your valuable contribution.

To the beautiful Goddesses Astarte, Shakti, Nidhana, and to the beautiful Gods, Shiva, Tony A, Martin, Ken Law, and E.T.R. who were my models for the pictures in books and the DVDs.

To all my tantric massage clients, both male and female. Thank you for your trust, respect, and responsiveness. To my friends and clients Dr S.H. and Dr A.E.

To my dear mentor Paul Haley who believed in me, nudging me in the right direction and always supporting me. Special thanks to F.C., amazing photographer and most generous friend. Also, a special thanks to K.F.S. who created such amazingly beautiful artwork for the book.

To my dear friends and students A.M., Cathy H., Shambhavi Krishan Shiva Kaur Rose, and J.S., who patiently helped me with the English language and editing – a major task indeed.

Deep gratitude to my dear friend S.J., who helped with valuable suggestions about structuring the book. Deep gratitude to Richard B., who has cast an expert eye on the manuscript.

To Joseph Kramer PhD, the 'Grandfather' of erotic massage and a kind human being, for your inspiring pioneering work (www.eroticmassage.com) and for the DVD testimonial.

To the wealth of knowledge and scientific research freely shared at www.reuniting.info.

To the pioneering work of Kenneth Ray Stubbs.

To Larry Clapp for your book *Prostate Health in 90 Days Without Drugs or Surgery.*

To my eager students wanting to have the complete manuscript and an easy reference to learn from.

And to all my gurus, lovers, and teachers.

Thank you. This book is a reality thanks to you all.

INTRODUCTION

Welcome and thank you for being open to exploring the art of honouring sacred sexuality. This book was written to share with you the profound teachings, practices, and life-affirming benefits of tantric healing massage and also to help educate our society in the ways of tantra.

In this book I share with you techniques to bring bliss, healing, and pleasure into your life and the lives of the people you touch. Tantric healing massage is an act of worship and a devotional practice that weaves together sexuality and spirituality.

This book will provide you with profound tools that will enhance your intimate relationships and help you to honour and worship the divine within your love partner through sacred touch, generosity of intention, and tantric rituals. The book was written to both partners, and both roles of the giver and the receiver.

All aspects of our lives are affected by relationships. Even in the business world we develop relationships. Being a fantastic lover is not all about sex. It is a spiritual journey. It is an art form with practices that are thousands of years old. I will take you through a journey of discovery, learning how to be a truly fantastic lover and perfect the art of worshiping your lover. 'There are a thousand ways to make love with a woman. If you add sex, you have a thousand and one.' (http://thesacredfemale.wordpress. com/2011/06/09/the-bible-and-female-ejaculatory-orgasms/)

Tantric healing massage is a combination of healing and erotic massage that has an emphasis on honouring the body of the God or the Goddess lying in front of you. The body is perceived as divine and is regarded as the temple of the soul. Tantric massage creates expansion on all levels of your being, enabling you to relax into a state of orgasmic plateau or erotic trance. The whole body is experienced as erotic, creating higher orgasmic states and an energy charge over the whole of the body, not just the genitals. It is a dance of energy, of giving and receiving, a joint meditation through touch. It touches the core of our being, the soul.

The practical massage sequence expands and frees energy over the whole body. As a result of following this sequence, people experience basking in an oceanic feeling, riding waves of bliss. People describe the feeling they experience as a taste of grace descending. You may touch spaciousness that is beyond time and space, as if you are space itself.

Tantric massage is communication through touch. Touch nourishes the body and the soul, and it quietens the mind. It enables a profound healing to take place naturally and effortlessly. Through this book, you will learn to use touch with sensitivity and awareness. This is a practical book that I assume you will be putting into practice. This is not a medical textbook; hence there will be very few medical terms used.

The first draft was written in 2009 when my husband went to India on a spiritual pilgrimage. I had so much energy and channelled it into writing four books. Whilst looking through the thousands of pictures, I had the idea of making a DVD and wanted it to be a surprise on his return. The DVD is available for sale, and now is the time to bring the book into being.

This book is a gift to my husband, my children, and the world. I offer it so that we can change and embrace all aspects of our being and celebrate healthy sexuality as it permeates all aspects of our life. This book is not suitable for all people. It is for open-minded people who are willing to explore new realms and transcend above the mundane, propelling their sexuality to new heights.

The book could be used in various ways. You can follow a sequence or study particular aspects in depth. You can follow all the teachings and explanations, which will provide you with a wide range of skills and knowledge, or you can dip in and skip to the bits you find most interesting. You will benefit either way, although it will be most effective if you integrate the teachings and practices into your life.

There are tantric secrets shared within this book. Some are implicit, and a couple of profound gems are hidden within the text, as is the tradition in ancient authentic tantric teachings. I hope you find them easily. It will depend on your readiness to rise to new levels of awareness.

I invite you to read this book and explore the practices shared. There may be some who will be challenged by some of the ideas shared here. You may wish to take on board all or just some of the concepts and practices presented. Experiment and explore for yourself and observe the outcome. Tantra is a journey of discovery and a science. It is the journey that is important to be savoured. Take what speaks to you; leave what doesn't. But most of all, enjoy the journey you are about to embark on.

Namaste , I salute the divinity within you.

Hanna Katz-Jelfs, Maha Shakti Kali Ma

WHY DO I NEED TANTRA?

Studying this book will enable you to:

- reach intimacy easily, even within a few minutes of practice.

- reawaken and rekindle the spark of love and sexuality in a long-term relationship that may have fallen into the 'familiarity and taken for granted' trap.

- channel erotic energy and integrate sexual energy into an erotic trance, riding the waves of bliss.

- enter an erotic trance state.

- use tantric massage to bond and enhance relationships and deepen intimacy.

- experience whole-being and whole-body orgasms.

- create healing.

- discover practical methods to connect, heal, and transform.

- transmit confidence with touch as a form of tactile communication.

- integrate sexuality and genitals into the whole being.

- discover the ability to worship the sacredness of the body with your hands.

- know about female ejaculation.

- understand male ejaculation control.

- know the truth about the female 'G-spot'.

- know the truth about the male 'G-spot'.

- know about the 'love muscles'.

- harness sexual energy in sex magic for manifestation and healing.

- integrate sexuality and spirituality.

- enhance your skills as a practitioner.

DISCLAIMER AND HEALTH WARNING

THIS BOOK CONTAINS SEXUALLY explicit material for educational purpose only and is not to be bought or viewed by minors. It is for those aged eighteen years and over only. All people involved in the making of the book and the DVDs were over the age of eighteen.

All the techniques and procedures shown in the books and the DVDs produced in the Tantric Sex Mastery series are believed to be safe. Neither the author of this book nor anyone associated with the production or distribution of this book and the DVDs can be held liable for any injury, physical or emotional, sustained directly or indirectly, however caused, arising from the practice of anything taught or demonstrated here.

All actions and responsibility lie with the giver and receiver only. You must check if there are any contraindications, for example, in case of blood clots, not to move them as this can be fatal. We would recommend avoiding massage completely if you are under the influence of drugs or alcohol or if you have any contagious or infectious disease, fever, recent operation, neuritis, or skin disease.

If you have any of the following conditions, it may be fine to proceed with the massage, provided affected areas are not touched: undiagnosed lumps, sunburn, cuts, abrasions, varicose veins, bruising, or undiagnosed pain. Professional medical advice should be sought.

Please consult a doctor prior to a massage if you have any of the following conditions: cancer, circulatory problems, cardiovascular conditions, pregnancy, high blood pressure, osteoporosis, emotional neurological neurosis, epilepsy, diabetes, asthma, bronchitis, psoriasis, eczema, oedema, acute rheumatism, arthritis, kidney infection, Bell's palsy, trapped or pinched nerves, gynaecological infections, HIV, AIDS, or any other medical condition being treated by a medical practitioner.

You are responsible for your own wellbeing. Take full responsibility for your own conduct. This book is intended to be used as a guideline only, and the author will not be held responsible for any actions or the experiences of individuals. Each person's experience will differ, and it may take time to reach the level of pleasure you seek. While the book cannot guarantee immediate results, your sincere intention, practice, and application will ultimately reward you immeasurably.

If there is any history of sexual abuse, please make sure you are seeking professional help and are emotionally equipped to deal with any psychological issues that may arise. Please ensure you avoid the use of alcohol and drugs for at least twelve hours prior to the tantric healing massage session. As you are working with profound energies, the brain creates many chemicals that are experienced as natural opiates, and you can become high with the energies released.

Due to the sensitive nature of this work, the names of individuals who have written in with testimonials have been withheld and shall remain confidential.

Tantric healing massage will change your life. Use it with awareness and respect, and enjoy the blessings.

Chapter 1:

What Is Tantra?

Tantra

Means practices.

Tantra is a cosmology.

It is embodied spirituality.

Tantra is the yoga of relationship,

The art of honouring sacred sexuality,

Awakening to aliveness to realize oneness,

Harnessing sexual energy as a gateway into enlightenment,

Celebrating and honouring the body as the temple and vehicle of your soul,

Stimulating total awareness of one's individuality within an all-encompassing cosmos.

Tantra is letting go of the ego, the illusions, and attachments of the self into the

Connection with all that is, remembering who we really are.

Tantra is a cosmology where the whole macrocosm is

Reflected within the microcosm of the body,

Every aspect of human expression used

As a portal or a meditation to

Reaching transcendence,

Experiencing ecstasy,

Bliss, and

Grace.

1

Tantric Formula: Orgasm + Consciousness in
the Power of Love = Tantric Magic

Tantra is a path of enlightenment that predates all the world's established religions. It is a way of being. It is not a religion or a set of beliefs. It is an embodied spirituality.

Tantra is also described as 'liberation through expansion', or weaving together energy and consciousness. Tantra is vast and comprises many traditions, and practices may vary. Some say we gravitate toward teachings that are perfect for us at each point in our journey, even though we may not appreciate it at the time. If you are reading this, you are ready to transcend the ordinary and the mundane and enter into a new realm.

In Sanskrit, the sacred language of India and Tibet, words may have several meanings. One of the meanings of the word 'tantra' is 'practices'. Yoga is an offshoot of tantra. In 1963 Sri Swami Satyananda Saraswati, the founder of the Bihar School of Yoga, the first university of yoga, said, 'Tantra is the mother; yoga is the son.' Yoga is a part of tantra that is concerned with body preparation and purification. But tantra is much more than that. It is also the yoga of relationships!

Tantra is a spiritual path for self-actualization or realizing unity or oneness with the divine. Some people prefer to call it nature, the universe, all that is, or God. The methods employed directly cultivate intimate relationships and enable us to engage with the world as it truly is. My particular style of tantra is the path of commitment – commitment to the self and to the love-partner. Even ascetic tantra, sometimes called white tantra (for those who are celibate and do not engage in intimate physical relationships), is concerned with relationships – inner relationships and a relationship with a guru. Red tantra is the spiritual path that consciously utilizes sexual energy and sensuality.

Tantra has appeared, and continues to appear, in many cultures throughout time. In the United Kingdom are pubs called the Green Man, the Ivy King, the Holly King, and the Oak King. These are remnants of the Druids' tradition and mark the seasons. There are many pubs in the United Kingdom that still bear these names, and they are the last reminders of a tradition that was connected to nature and the land, and we may name this as the Celtic tantra. The legend of Robin Hood is another remnant of Celtic tantra. Stonehenge is an ancient historical site in the south of England United Kingdom. It is connected to the Druids and the seasons, and it is a national heritage site. Rites and ceremonies were carried out on this site. Dr Terence Meaden, an expert on Stonehenge, is often interviewed about the secrets of the stones. It is a place of union, where the feminine powers and the masculine energies are thought to merge at certain times of the year. The shadow cast from the tallest (phallic) pillar penetrates perfectly into the stone circles (the womb) precisely at the first light of Midsummer Day.

Alchemy was part of the tantric path in medieval Europe. Usually thought of as transforming base metal into gold, alchemy was concerned with transforming raw sexual energy into refined expressions of humanity. Later, alchemy evolved into chemistry as we now know it. The Kabbalah is the Jewish tantra, and the Tao is the Chinese tantra. Zen in the Far East and Sufism in the Middle East, predating Islam, are also varieties of tantra.

In his article on the tantra exhibition at the Hayward Gallery forty years after the first public tantra exhibition at the Hayward Gallery in London, Martin Jelfs wrote:

Eccentric characters such as Pierre Bernard, the Omnipotent Oom, founded the Tantrik Order of America in 1905 and later set up Tantra and yoga clubs where tantric meditation and some sexual practices were taught. In Britain, there has always been some tradition of tantric practices, mixed up with the mystery schools of meditation and the pagan and sex magic traditions with characters such as Alistair Crowley. (http://www.tantra.uk.com/HaywardGallery.html)

Tantra has always existed in the West through paganism, the mystery traditions, the hidden knowledge, and through esoteric understanding. Even the symbol of the British Medical Association, the caduceus (the staff with entwined serpents ascending it and wings at the top), is full of tantric symbolism. The caduceus shows the ascent of kundalini energy up the central channel and the paths of Ida and Pingala. The latter are the intertwining snakes on the left and the right, representing the male and female, the sun and the moon. At the third eye in the middle of the forehead, they unite and take off in spiritual flight.

Tantra as a spiritual technique has a deeply intuitive as well as consciously studied knowledge of the human body, both its natural anatomy and its more ethereal subtle qualities.

Tantra differs from other spiritual paths in the acceptance and celebration of the body, the senses, sexuality, and feelings. It uses methods and practices to help us evolve spiritually and to embrace and integrate all aspects of our being in order to enjoy more fulfilling relationships.

Image 04: Heart Meditation

Traditionally, tantra was practiced by the wealthy who were fortunate to have spare time and resources. The Buddha taught the rich and the educated, as they had the physical and mental capacity to absorb the teachings, whereas a starving person, fighting for survival, is not likely to be receptive to transpersonal teachings that will help him transcend. This is not a cultural or traditions discourse, but simply acknowledges that globally and across cultures, an individual who is starving may not have the capacity for self-realization or transpersonal matters, but rather concentrates on basic survival.

The most succinct definitions of tantra are 'awakening to aliveness to realize oneness' and 'embodied spirituality'. These definitions encapsulate the methods and the whole purpose and intention of tantra. It is concerned with practice meditations on death and letting go. Tantra includes meditations on the death of the ego, preparation for dying, dissolving the illusion of self, and realizing the connection with all that is. At the same time, tantra is concerned with living in the here and now, embodying the temple of your soul, which is your body.

Tantra utilizes every aspect of our lives and human expression as a gateway to self-realization. It is an opportunity to realize who you really are by searching, experiencing, and looking from within. The tantric path may challenge your relationships and your world constructs. Tantra is the path of Vajrayana Buddhism, meaning the 'thunderbolt lightning path', which is the fastest path to enlightenment in this lifetime.

Bliss is a state of being that can easily be attained through practices of tantric healing massage. It is a state that can be recognized in the smile of the Buddha, mirrored in the compassionate gaze of the Madonna and the enlightened serenity of the saints depicted in tantric art. Bliss can be experienced as a euphoric state, ecstatic joyfulness, deep silence, or contentment descending on you.

Tantra is a profound way of life that embraces sexuality and all aspects of human expression. Tantra teaches us how to celebrate our sensuality and how to harness raw sexual energy, transforming that energy into a more refined, creative expression for our own benefit and that of the wider world.

Tantra is a most extraordinary path. It amplifies what is already there, acting as a magnifying glass. At the same time, it teaches miraculous techniques to propel your life to a transcendent level, where you become a divine human being, a living god or goddess, right here, right now, experiencing heaven on earth. Tantra is the meeting place of paradoxes, when two extremes are present at the same time. This is tantra, with bliss in the middle, where you can feel full and empty at the same time, where you can experience time dilation, where time stands still or passes very fast, when five minutes feel like five hours, and when five hours feel like five minutes.

Testimonial

> I felt like I was walking on air the rest of today, and remarkably, time really seemed to stand still for me! (B.L.)

Some books are tantric and have no mention of sex. The Dalai Lama practices tantra. Tantra is vast and diverse. If there were a goal in tantra, it would be to reunite with or realize the divine nature of oneness, dissolving into all that is, experiencing bliss or clarity

Tantra is very interested in harnessing the power of sexuality, using it as a doorway into enlightenment or opening into the universe that is within each of us. Tantra is latent potential power that waits to be awakened; it is our birth right, after all.

Tantric healing massage is often misunderstood. The word 'tantra' is already highly charged and has many connotations and misinterpretations. What makes the difference is setting out the intentions, and the process you will learn here will create the 'magic' that happens during the session and afterward. Some who belittle and make jokes about tantra often do so because they have feelings of inadequacy and are uncomfortable with their own sexuality. They may have misconceptions about tantra, and criticism and sarcastic putdowns often mask their ignorance and insecurity. They may feel threatened by the notion of tantra or sexuality itself.

A Google search for the word tantra produced twenty-four million hits. According to Martin Jelfs:

> It has become the hobby of pop stars and on many parts of the internet, something that looks rather like porn and sexual services. It seems that tantra has come from the obscure preserve of oriental scholars to a lifestyle accessory or a selling point in the great spiritual/cultural shopping mall of the internet.' (http://tantra.uk.com/HaywardGallery.html)

There are dictionaries that tell you Tantrism is a rather disreputable and disowned branch of Hindu spirituality. Then you are told that all

Tibetan Buddhism is tantric. There are innumerable Internet sites that seem to link tantra to endurance tests of sexual performance or as a way to enhance your love life or as a form of therapy. And as I mentioned previously, there are books on tantra where there is no mention of sex, even in the index.

In some of the thousands of books available, you may be told you have to have a guru to whom you are devoted and that it is a secret oral tradition. You may be told that the word simply means 'practices', and that tantra is a compilation of methods of meditation. Tantra can seem very obscure and small, and then you are told all yoga is part of tantra. Grasping tantra is rather like trying to get hold of soap in the bath; just when you think you have it in your grasp, it slips away.

Once again you find yourself seeking something that seems just on the edge of your fingertips, searching for clarity. Tantra can seem to be like the image of a tree – many roots under the ground and many branches overhead but only one simple solid trunk. The danger with tantra is that we make it what we want or fear it to be; and words lose their meanings in a postmodern soup of desires and fears, a sort of 'spiritual curry'.

CHAPTER 2:

What is Tantric Healing Massage?

Tantric healing massage is

A ritual of honouring

An art form

Using:

Touch,

Mantra,

Dedication,

Visualization,

Setting intentions,

Sublimation of energy,

Transmutation of kundalini,

Riding the wave of orgasmic bliss

Weaving of consciousness and energy

Through the listening hands we experience blissful orgasms.

Tantric healing massage enables you to experience awakened awareness and being totally aroused, energized, and relaxed at the same time. This could be thought of as a paradox, until you experience it.

In tantric healing massage, we touch the divine essence within us, feeling connected to all that is. There are no divisions at the core of your being, just total connectedness. The aim is to observe every minute detail of what is happening within and around you, yet in a totally calm relaxed way.

You will learn to transmute and sublimate the raw sexual energy into a refined flow of energy, moving it upwards towards the crown chakra at the top of the head, integrating and cultivating more awareness or consciousness. Chakras will be explained in a later chapter.

You will learn to move in a tantric way, with grace, merging energy and awareness, touching the body and embodying tantra into your being, cultivating the perception of oneness and non-duality.

You are invited to dance the dance of consciousness and enable awareness to move through you and through your whole being. It is a dance of energy and consciousness, where erotic energy is the medium flowing in the body and bliss is the orgasmic expression. Here, all is divine and all expression of our existence is welcomed in a non-judgmental way.

Tantric healing massage is the weaving together of energy, using mantra, awareness and intention, and quality of touch, honouring yourself and others. A tantric practitioner should have a daily tantric practice comprising of a yoga sequence, sets of mantras (chants), mudras (gestures), meditations, and yantras (sacred geometric symbols for meditation).

Tantric massage is a ritual of honouring. It is a wonderful practice for honouring your partner as a divine being and honouring every single part of the body and being. When people avoid the genitals and sexuality, a split can be created in the psyche or the body. Tantric healing massage shows us that the entire body is sensual and that potentially we can be orgasmic in the whole of our being, not just the genitals. At that point everything is divine, including the genitals. The body is the temple of the soul. I call the genitals divine design.

In traditional tantra there is no such thing as tantric massage *per se*, it is one aspect of the healing arts to be mastered. The sixty-four temple healing arts also include flower arrangements, singing, and playing musical instruments.

Tantric healing massage is a dance of giving and receiving. It is the interplay of unconditional generosity and graceful acceptance. There is an expression in the Jewish Kabbalah, *Ki Netinah Kamoha KeKabbalah*, which means 'for giving is receiving.'

LESS IS MORE!

The more subtle the energy you become accustomed to and learn to enjoy and experience, the more pleasure you can get from everything, even the wind blowing as if it is singing or caressing your body, making love to your whole being. Through the 'listening hands' we can experience blissful orgasms on all levels of our being.

Tantric healing massage is very much the opposite of sadomasochism, where more stimulation is needed to recreate original excitation. Sensitivity will come with practice, and practice, as you know, is tantra.

The body and its subtle maps of the flows of energy are the deep principles of tantra. It uses the subtlety of duality: masculine and feminine, yang and yin, Shiva and Shakti, method and wisdom to transcend duality. A primary emphasis in tantra is the transmuting or sublimation of sexual energy to fuel spiritual attainment rather than its release in sexual pleasure.

Traditional tantra sexualizes ritual, whereas modern neo-tantra ritualizes sex. Traditional tantra views the whole of the world as the dance of male and female principals and the whole of the universe represented in our being.

Tantric massage can enable and propel the enlightenment process by giving a taste of bliss or ecstasy beyond the body and ordinary reality. Enlightenment is a self-realization or self-actualization. Samadhi is one of the states of highest consciousness realized. If there was a purpose for tantra, then it would be a state of bliss or unity with all that is. There are many paradoxes in tantra, such as the perception of the universe as being empty and full at the same time.

Tantric healing massage is about interweaving Shakti energy and Shiva consciousness. Shakti is normally the feminine embodiment, the dynamic principle, whilst Shiva is the masculine expression, the latent potential in the realms of the un-manifested. (See the next chapter on Shiva and Shakti.)

Main Intentions of a Tantric Healing Massage

1. To honour you and your partner on all levels of your being: physical, emotional, psychological, intellectual, and spiritual.

2. To facilitate healing on all levels of your being.

3. To enable you to experience erotic trance or orgasmic plateau.

4. To enable both men and women to experience multiple orgasms.

5. To enable you to experience bliss and enlightenment, being at **one** with **all that is**.

Testimonial

> I just wanted to say thank you again for a truly blissful experience on Tuesday. You filled me with your energy - physically, sexually, emotionally and spiritually. I still have not come down from the place that you took me to. I have been following your teaching and guidance ever since. I feel honoured and privileged. I felt as though my soul was joined, with a circuit of energy pulsing through me. I felt I was in a place where I was meant to be, and I wanted to stay there forever.' (AG)

THE THREE DIRECTIONS OF TANTRIC HEALING MASSAGE

Tantric healing massage can evolve in different directions as it unfolds naturally through the process. It can become an expanded pleasure experience or can become healing or it can result in tasting bliss or even enlightenment.

1. **Expanded pleasure.** You can experience a phenomenon called 'riding the waves of bliss', extended orgasms and multiple orgasms for both women and men. This is the easiest state to experience and is easily accessible to all, as human beings desire and seek pleasure.

2. **Healing** on all levels of our being – physical, emotional, psychological, intellectual, and spiritual. Healing is a side effect of tantric healing massage, though sometimes a particular issue may be targeted consciously, or an issue may arise during the process which is then ready to be healed and dispersed.

3. **Bliss or enlightenment** can be the ultimate state to attain when individuals are seeking spiritual fulfilment. Tantric healing massage propels the enlightenment process through states of bliss or provides you with tastes of natural ecstatic

states that arise from connection to the joy of your soul and a sense of deep knowledge of our true nature. This state is experienced when we let go and dissolve into all that is, surrendering ourselves completely.

PREVIEW OF THE SUCCESS RECIPE

Here is a preview of the summary of successful tantric massage intentional ingredients, which will be expanded on later in the book:

1. Presence

2. Honouring all levels of your being

3. Intention and invocation

4. Healing on all levels of your being

5. Riding the waves of bliss: orgasmic plateau/erotic trance

6. EMO – extended massive orgasm, multi-orgasmic wo/men

7. Dedication and manifesting your vision using sex magic

8. Enlightenment, self-realization, bliss

CHAPTER 3:

Embodying the God and the Goddess

SHIVA AND SHAKTI

THE ROLE OF THE god and the goddess, Shiva and Shakti, is primary in tantra. People are regarded as embodying the god and the goddess. Each of us embodies both male and female aspects, and the many deities that are used in tantric symbolism represent different aspects of our selves.

Shiva is the masculine aspect or the god in the Hindu tradition. Shakti is the feminine aspect of ourselves and is the goddess. Shakti means 'woman', the goddess, radiance. Her essence is energy and sound. Shakti also means 'phenomena', everything that changes, a whirlwind storm, thoughts, feelings, emotions, and experiences.

Shiva means 'man', the god, masculinity. He is the embodiment of consciousness, awareness, presence, discernment or discrimination without judgment. Shiva represents everything that never changes – presence, awareness, essence, and spaciousness, all that is. It is timeless, beyond space and time.

In tantra, Shakti traditionally is the initiator. Therefore she gives first to Shiva. Shakti is the creative energy, but without Shiva consciousness, Shakti could be experienced as destructive power. Tantra acknowledges that the man, as Shiva, needs to embody the masculine quality of presence in order to allow the feminine to let go into trust. It is the main key to tantric massage. Weaving Shakti energy with Shiva consciousness is the ultimate union.

In tantra, Shiva is the very foundation of the platform upon which Shakti, femininity, can have her beautiful dance. Without Shiva's platform or his witnessing Shakti's dance of life, she cannot radiate her brilliance, her essence. This is depicted in tantric imagery, where the goddess dances on the reclining figure of Shiva, the god. He is in deep meditation, helping Shakti the goddess to dance the world into creative existence.

It is the polarities and the differences that make the attractions and the magnetism or chemistry. This can also be observed in same-gender couples. One partner embodies masculine qualities, while the other will assume the feminine aspects and they are comfortable at changing their roles as needed. We all have both masculine and feminine qualities within us.

The image we use of the pole dancer as Shakti illustrates the relationship of the masculine and feminine aspects. Shakti can perform the most amazing dance and twirling. Shiva represents the pole that enables her to give her best performance. Shiva, masculinity, represents consciousness, the platform upon which life and creation plays. Shiva is all 'that which never changes'. Shiva's awareness brings balance and the ability to see through the turbulent emotional dramas of life and experiences. The phenomena, everything that changes, thoughts, feelings, emotions, stories, are all Shakti's play, and the dance of the goddess, which occurs within Shiva's consciousness, is space itself.

Shiva's awareness is the pure consciousness that can support all of life's play. It provides the clarity of awareness that contains all within it. The Tibetan tradition has a wonderful sky-gazing meditation that helps realize the transient nature of all things – phenomena, feeling, thoughts, emotions, or Shakti. She is like the clouds and Shiva is space.

In tantra there is neither a 'positive' nor a 'negative' experience. In tantra there is no 'good' or 'bad' feelings, as these would be judgments.

Whatever the experience is, it just **is**. Like a tree, it is neither a good nor a bad tree, it is just 'treeing'. It is perfect just as it is. The highest teachings are that all is perfect just as it is.

Tantra is the marriage of the feminine dynamic principle of Shakti, and the pure still awareness of Shiva consciousness. Tantra is the ultimate union of the interplay of these two seemingly opposing principles in our lives. In yoga, it is acknowledged that the union of Shiva and Shakti occurs within our own bodies, integrating our masculine and feminine selves, realizing oneness or wholeness.

It felt really perfect … and it feels good to commit to a series of sessions with you working in this way. There were several aaaaaaaaah-ha moments during and after the session, and I look forward to continuing to work with the idea of a powerful yin. I also realize that what I have been on the search for a very long time is the presence of yang … which I have had confused with wanting a relationship. (D.G.)

Image 05: Couple in *Yub Yum*

SPIRITUAL STORY

This modern interpretation of a traditional Tibetan and Kabbalist short story has been used by teachers to illustrate the essence of human divinity.

God, who is beyond gender, asked the helpers, 'Where can I hide from mankind? Humanity is trying to capture me and destroy my essence.'

One helper said, 'Hide in the Himalayas. Man shall never find you there.'

God thought about it and said, 'One day, man will create warm clothes and strong walking boots. He will come up the mountain, stick vending machines on me, and destroy my essence.'

Another helper said, 'Hide in the depth of the sea. Man shall never reach you there.'

God thought about it and said, 'One day man will build a great big fish of metal. He will come down and seek me. He will capture me on film and destroy my essence.'

Another helper said, 'Hide on the moon. Man shall never reach you there.'

God thought about it and said, 'One day man will build great big birds of metal. He will land and play golf on me, stick flags in me, bring me down to earth in rocks, and destroy my essence.'

Another helper said, 'Hide in the heart of man. He shall never think to look in there.'

'God' sees through your eyes, feels through your touch and speaks through your mouth.

CHAPTER 4:

The Importance of Obtaining a Clear Consent

N o one will have a profound healing experience if they have not come to know that they are in a situation where their boundaries will be respected and that they will be held in safety as they let themselves go. We have an ethical duty to care for people who surrender themselves to our touch, and it is imperative that you get four variants of consent.

1. The first form of consent involves asking out loud and negotiating terms prior to touch commencing. Even with love partners that have been together a long time, you will still need to negotiate what the tantric massage will involve.

2. The second form of agreement is energetic, during the massage, where the receiver may have entered an altered state of conciseness. Bring your awareness into your own being, noticing your own feelings. Have the intention of being a clear channel for healing energy. The giver asks internally, 'Would it be beneficial for (use their name), if I do (specify what it is you intend to carry out). Wait for a clear 'yes', otherwise continue the massage without carrying out the proposed action. Some people feel the answer, some hear it, and others see it or get a definite sense of knowing.

3. The third form of consent is a felt response through the body. The receiver may have said yes, but if the body starts contracting, you need to be aware he or she has become resistant. This can come up at any time and may result in emotional expression.

4. The fourth form of consent is required before you begin to massage the genitals. No matter what has been agreed beforehand, you need to ask specifically if the receiver wants the massage to continue to his or her genitals, and you need to hear a definite 'yes' spoken. 'Hum' or 'ahh' is not sufficient to grant permission to touch the genitals.

CHAPTER 5:

Bringing Consciousness to Touch

THE LISTENING HANDS

There are three main ways in which we can touch another:

1. A person can touch the other the way they themselves wish to touch. This could be experienced as a form of taking, and it is how not to touch. Be mindful. This could be experienced as abusive or violating, even though the giver thinks they are acting compassionately. Even when a receiver feels they have enjoyed a touch, once they have had an opportunity to reflect and replay events, they may come to feel shame or even reawaken a repressed memory of abuse. Notice their breathing and reactions so that you feel what is appropriate.

2. Alternatively, a person can touch the way the receiver would like to be touched. You can take time to ask and understand exactly how the other desires to be touched. This is a great thing to do when learning the art of honouring touch. It is important to seek feedback so that the receiver feels heard and listened to. If you do this exercise before a massage, it will help the receiver to be more receptive and open to your touch. This will help you both to discover healthy boundaries and wishes, and it will empower the receiver to be more assertive and learn to express their desires. This

element of Shiva consciousness goes to creating the safe space for Shakti essence to open, dance, and flow.

3. The third way of touching is called 'listening hands'. It is the experience of being totally present, of being attuned to the other. You take yourself out of the way and are totally there for the receiver in whatever arises, being present for the receiver and touching in a way that your higher self knows, tuning into their body. The receiver's body will communicate. Allow yourself to sense how they want and need to be touched. This awareness can occur only when you let go of any agenda of your own or any expectations on how the session may turn out to be and when you are completely present for the other.

This subtle language of touch, the art of conscious touch, is fundamental to tantric healing massage. It is a form of expressive touch where you, the giver, are a musician, an artist playing a rare and most precious instrument of divine music. This is the art of honouring touch and sacred sexuality.

Testimonial

A very sincere 'thank you' for that fantastic session. It exceeded my expectations (which were high to begin with), and I can't wait to repeat the experience, a paying tribute to your skills! They are certainly both life- and energy-enhancing. (B.M.)

THE CONTINUUM OF TOUCH

There are three main parts to the continuum of touch according to Martin Jelfs.

The First

Instrumental. Lots of childhood touch; moving, feeding, cleaning, restraining, punishing.

Playful or tickling. Could be experienced as playful or invasive and abusive.

Affirming. Positive experience, usually in good childhood experiences; comforting, reassuring, connecting.

Sensual. Sensitizing, relaxing, awakening.

The Second

Culture divides at this point.

Erotic. Awakens some excitement in the other.

Sexual. Generally part of intimate human contact.

Genitals touching. Could be experienced as comforting, stimulating sexual energy to move, arousing, reassuring.

The Third

This is the point where tantric body work divides.

Mutual genital contact. Symmetry so roles are more easily lost; may concentrate arousal in the genitals rather than spread. It is more like a usual habit and therefore does not constitute a therapeutic form of touch.

HEALING RELEASES

The expression of an emotional reaction during a session may be a sign that trauma is being released either in a vocal expression or in energy responses, as well as peristalsis, which is a movement released in the gastrointestinal tract that makes gurgling sounds.

Trauma is stored in the body. Tissue has memory, and until it is released with awareness, the cells will regenerate with the same memory, thus carrying on the trauma and associations. The subconscious and the body will release memories if ever they are touched or some situation arises that triggers a reaction, as though the experience is being relived.

Many people suppress past difficulties by employing substances such as alcohol or drugs or by addictive behaviours. This can be effective in the short term, though it uses a lot of emotional and mental energy. However, the human makeup is such that there is a fundamental striving for the greater. Therefore, trauma may surface as a way of propelling growth.

As you have both Shakti and Shiva attributes regardless of your gender, you can call on your masculine or feminine attributes, conscious or creative qualities when appropriate. When an emotional release occurs for the receiver, you as the giver will need to embody Shiva consciousness. It will be clear to you how to respond. It may be appropriate to stop and be a still strong presence for a while, or it may be appropriate to continue enabling the receiver to go into an even deeper release. Through tantric healing therapy and psychotherapy, trauma can be resolved.

Case History

A client upon arrival shared that he had been looking at my website for some years. Alerted by this statement, I asked what made him decide to see me now. He insisted he just wanted to experience the massage. I asked him what had happened during that week. He said nothing at first. He then divulged that his mother had died the previous week and that he was very close to her. He then added that his father had Alzheimer's and he had just transferred him to an institution to care for him. He continued to share that his wife had left him and taken the children away to another country. During the treatment I placed a hand on his side to connect, and he overreacted, even though it was a gentle touch. He shared that was where his gallbladder was removed five years before in the same hospital bed where his mother just died. I had to respond, changing the format of the session in order to support his emotional state.

It is therefore very important when giving a tantric healing massage to be conscious and aware of the receiver's unspoken and subconscious responses. You can then adjust the touch and the massage according to what would be for the best interest of the recipient in response to what is arising in the session.

EMBODYING AWARENESS

During the massage, you will need to embody awareness, presence, and the intention of honouring. Touch the body with the intention of honouring. It is sometimes described as playing a magic divine musical instrument, such as the *rudra veena*, a rare tantric instrument similar to a sitar with two gaud chambers. Hold the awareness and the intention of reverence, as if it is the first time you have touched this being, even if it is the 108th time you have done so. What you focus on is what you achieve.

Testimonial

> You helped me enormously. I do feel a shift has taken place within me thanks to you and your inspired teaching, healing, your dedication, sincerity and warm heart. It's God's work you are doing; bless you. (E.)

CHAPTER 6:

Physical and Energy Anatomy

EROGENOUS ZONES

T ANTRA KRIYA YOGA MAPS three major categories of erogenous zones over the whole of the body – the tertiary, secondary, and primary zones.

As a general rule, the first areas to be touched are the tertiary erogenous zones. They are the most receptive and the least sensitive. These are the areas furthest from the genitals, breasts, and mouth, and honouring them allows the receiver to relax into the experience. The areas at the back of the heart chakra and between the shoulder blades are subtly connected to the genitals through the energy channels in the body.

The secondary erogenous zones are more sensitive. They include the upper lip, under the nose, the left side of the neck for women and the right side of the neck for men, the inner thighs, the back of the knees, and the inside of the wrists.

The primary erogenous zones are touched last, after the whole body has been prepared, as they are most sensitive. If these areas are approached too soon without emotional and physical preparation, it may be experienced as a turn off or even cause the receiver to close down. This certainly affects love relationships and has traumatized many women. In extreme cases, it can cause vaginismus, a vaginal contraction that causes discomfort and pain and prevents penetration.

The primary erogenous zones are the genitals and all the natural orifices: the mouth, the nipples, the rectum, the ears, nostrils, and navel. The sensitivity in these areas varies greatly. Some people are not sensitive in the navel, whereas others are super-sensitive. Approach with great respect the breasts, the yoni (the vulva), the vajra (penis), and the gateway to heaven (anus). We are all unique and divine.

Back of the Knee

The back of the knee, or the knee pit, is the *popliteal fossa*. It is highly sensitive. It is not so commonly acknowledged, undervalued yet highly erotic.

Cheek Bones

There are many acupressure points on the cheek bones. Cheek bones are most alluring. They are the instant and most prevalent visual display of sexuality. Women try to replicate the way they look during and after love making, where they radiate and are most attractive with the afterglow on their rosy cheeks.

Mouth and Lips

The mouth is regarded as the upper yoni, the Hindu term for vagina, meaning the sacred source of all. There are many nerve endings that are connected with the mouth, and they directly affect our sexual response. In love making, often the woman wants or feels as if she needs to be kissed.

The tongue is a master switch in tantra yoga. It helps connect and switch between energy channels within the body. Touching tongues can create electricity between lovers. Saliva is also used for healing. When people are wounded, licking the place helps the healing process and cleans the wound.

Lips are highly arousing for a woman. The use of lipstick is an unconscious attempt to replicate the colouring which happens naturally when the blood rushes and engorges their lips during love making, making them even more attractive. The lips of the mouth and the rosy cheeks are some of the primary ways that the human animal can tell if a woman is ready for intimacy.

In intimate lovers' massage, massaging the inside of the mouth is important.

Eyes

The eyes are said to be the doorway to the soul. Energy comes out through the eyes. People communicate much through the eyes, consciously and unconsciously, with staring piercing looks, love, hostility, lust, a whole range of emotions.

Pupil dilation can indicate states of arousal, as well as the direction of eyes and the level of the eye lids. There is a lot of knowledge regarding the eyes and what they communicate. This is used by television advertising campaigns to influence consumers and by NLP (neurolinguistic programming). Moods and expressions are mainly conveyed via the eyes.

When we are aroused, many of us shut our eyes. It is a tantric practice to keep your eyes open when you make love with the beloved. Allow yourself to be seen and witnessed in your sensuality and arousal. This will liberate and bring more intimacy. As was said in the comedy film *The Guru*, 'In To Me You See.'

Ears

The ears are highly erotic. They have many energy points, and they are sensitive. Inserting a finger into the ear can result in hearing the sounds of life within you, hearing the oceans of your own being!

Neck

The neck and throat are very important. It is where energy lines change the flow and pathway from the body, flowing either side of the *shushumna*, left and right of the central channel to the back and front of the head. It is analogous to a water valve. When energy is not flowing freely, the mind and body are experienced as split, and some can inhabit their heads yet not be grounded in the body, and vice versa.

In the throat reside the points for karma clearing and the father or masculine points.

During sexual arousal, the throat is a major player, and some people like to feel constriction in this area as it can heighten their sexual arousal, sometimes at the high cost of losing lives. We can bring awareness and lightly place fingers at the base of the neck and the underside of the chin to create heightened states in a safe and honouring act of transformation.

Skin and Hair

The skin is your largest physical organ. We are able to sense touch through the somato-sensory system, which is a vast web of touch receptors and nerve endings in the skin. There are many types; some sense texture, pressure; and vibration; some perceive heat; some sense pain; and some help us perceive our positioning in space and coordination in relation to the self. We do not have to be conscious of this. We are very fortunate to have a sophisticated human divine body that can take care of itself and allow our conscious mind to engage in activities to further our evolution and improve life on earth.

Touch is transferred via the skin and can be perceived as an erotic and sensual experience. Many people who go to the hairdresser's enjoy the head and neck massage. It is one of the erotic experiences that we are allowed and are encouraged to engage in publicly.

Remember the skin is your largest organ. It is not a sealing membrane, but it is a permeable breathing organ. Whatever you apply on the bare skin will be absorbed and transferred to the internal organs.

Hair is also important for conducting kundalini energy. Sikhs traditionally keep the hair long. Every single hair is affecting many nerve endings and tissue. This also applies to genital hair. As well as affecting many levels of tissue, having pubic hair looks mysterious and arousing.

The fashionable trend of removing pubic hair due to fear of the full-bodied feminine shapes has brought about a sanitized and unfeminine version of a woman. It may be infantilizing like a prepubescent child, removing any unconscious threats that a full feminine body may represent.

The ability to manipulate images has created idealised images of people; in real life, we will never look like the fantasy of the graphic designer. Please note, no images in this book have been digitally manipulated. All the people in the book and the DVDs are real people. They are perfect just as they are, beautiful divine beings.

Breasts

Most women have sensitivity regarding their breasts. When you approach the breasts, please be mindful that they is sensitive, and have respect. It is the feminine positive centre, the heart chakra. A woman gives from this centre. It would be highly advisable to prepare the body before reaching the breasts, so that the woman is more receptive. The ducts inside the breasts are connected to the uterus, and sucking on the nipples could bring a woman to an orgasm. After child-birth women are advised to breast-feed to help reduce the size of their belly.

Where the breasts are more pronounced or sensitive, it is best to cup the hands around the whole breast, just holding for a while and leaving the nipples free. With a firm touch, moving the breast in a slow rhythmic circle will feel reassuring, safe, and erotic. First touch the periphery before proceeding to the nipples.

Arms, Arm Pits, and Wrists

The hands are extensions of the heart. There are many points to be aware of in the palms of the hand regarding giving and receiving, breathing points.

The inside of the wrist is associated with the joy of the soul.

The inside of the elbow is regarded as the area to heal sorrow. The outside of the elbow is treated to help letting go.

Arm pits could be sensitive, and the receiver will need to be relaxed in order to be able to receive touch in areas that may be ticklish.

It can feel affirming and reassuring as well as sensual to massage the arms. Try various types of pressures from firm to feather-touch, and switch between them so you can feel the difference in the effect.

Fingers

The fingertips have many nerve endings. Very young children touch everything and move their fingers as they try to construct the new and exciting world.

There are healing modalities recognizing that the whole body, including the internal organs, is mapped on the fingers. In some healing modalities, the different segments and each finger are associated with different emotional states. The web between the fingers is also highly erotic.

Thighs and the Psoas Muscles

This muscle starts in the upper thigh and continues to the twelfth vertebra. The psoas muscle is located on the side of the lumbar lower back region of the spine or the vertebral column and the edge of the pelvis. It is joined by the iliacus muscles, and together they form the iliopsoas. There are three major meridians in the inner thighs that are worth paying attention to.

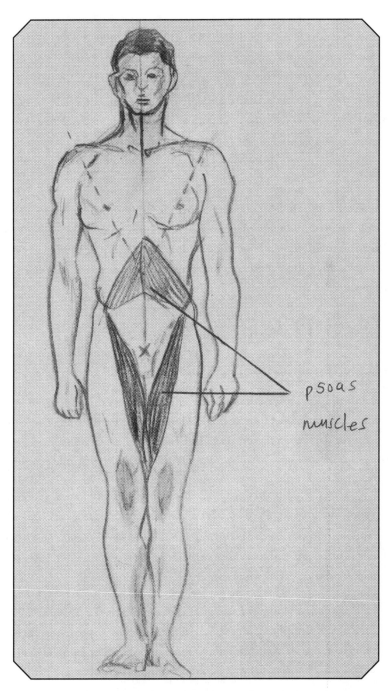

psoas
muscles

Image 06: Psoas Muscles

Ankles

Holding the ankles is a way to help the receiver feel grounded. The ankles are very important in tantric healing massage. The inner ankle bones are associated with the genitals in the acupuncture modality, and intuition in the colour-puncture healing modalities. The ankle bone is associated with self-love and acceptance and self-forgiveness, as well as being a site of erotic energy connected to the genitals.

Feet

Pay attention to the feet. They are most important. Some people may not feel the feet when they get cut off from their emotions. When energies begin to flow, people suddenly feel tingling in their feet. In reflexology, the whole body is mapped on the feet. Toes could also be highly erotic.

INTERNAL TANTRIC ORGANS

The Vagus Sensory Nerve

The vagus nerve, the tenth cranial nerve, is the wandering nerve; it meanders from the occiput through various organs and all the way to the genitals. It is comprised of about 90 per cent of sensory receptor neurons which relay sensory information back to the brain.

The vagus nerve controls the skeletal muscles and provides motor parasympathetic fibres to most of the organs from the neck to the colon. The parasympathetic system controls the ability to relax, digest, and also perform bodily excretions comprising urination, defecation, salivation, and tear production (lacrimation).

It is responsible for much of our reaction to stress and pleasure, and it is highly active in post-trauma stress situations. This very important nerve helps in understanding why some people react in a certain way and others differently to the same stimulus or event.

Day and Light

From the ninth to the eleventh day after their period has started, women are ovulating and have higher sexual appetite and are more likely to want sexual relations, including having affairs. Daylight arouses sexuality, whereas darkness supports the ability to experience shamanic journeying and dreaming. Nowadays, with artificial lighting and the over-stimulation from excessive media, advertising, sounds, and technology, we are less in touch with our natural rhythms.

There are benefits, however. Because we have artificial light, this allows us more hours of light and thus time to spend studying, reflecting, doing, and creating more and thus evolving more to a higher consciousness.

Subtle Anatomy

This image shows the energy points to be aware of.

Body part	Association
The centre of the palm	Self-healing point
The ring finger	Emotional attachments
The middle finger	Feelings
The end of the middle finger	Emotional healing
The top of the back and the root of the neck, where the cervical vertebrae end and the thoracic vertebrae begin is where the melancholy zone is located.	Melancholy zone, this area may be more pronounced when feeling sad. It is highly beneficial to massage this area.
The top of the shoulder blades	Opening to the divine
Between the shoulder blades – the back of the heart chakra	The genitals zone
The middle of the back	The life points
The lower back area	The relationship zone
The back of the heel	The Bardo point, Tibetan for the world between the worlds, helping overcome fear of death.
The elbows	Letting go of sorrow or other emotions
The inner wrist	Joy of the soul
Centre line on the back of the thighs	Emotional and physical detoxifying
Belly button	Mother's ancestral imprints
Throat	Changing Karma and Father's ancestral imprints
The inside of the ankles	Intuition, also connected with the genitals
The outside of the ankles	Self love and the genitals

Image 07: Subtle Anatomy Chart

CHAKRAS AND ENERGY IN THE BODY

There are twenty major meridians, energy lines in the body.

There are approximately 72,000 nadis, energy channels.

The chakras are the energy centres that are

The subtle doorways connecting

Between the ethereal and

The physical bodies.

There are at least 72,000 energy channels called 'nadis', in the body. These are energy lines similar to those that are activated in reflexology, where you can stimulate points on the feet which affect the internal organs and limbs. Reflexology originates from Ayurveda, the Indian science of longevity and health.

Testimonial

Another amazing experience was that of the power of the energy body and how it easily overcomes the physical. The grounding of the third eye and the crown was particularly important for the process. **Wow!** I would never have believed the power we were dealing with until I felt it physically!! It showed me I need to be very careful with it. (B.T.)

Chakras

The chakras are energy wheels, or vortexes, which are the subtle portals connecting the etheric body, which is the subtle and vital body in esoteric schools, and the physical body. In Sanskrit, 'chakra' means circle or energy centre. I refer to it as the 'spinning wheels of energy'.

There are different maps of the chakras depending on which system you use – the Hindu, Tao, Sufi, Tibetan, Mayan, African, Kabbalah, etc.

In the Hindu tradition (the most commonly used map), there are seven main chakras and one secret chakra. There are also 122 minor chakras. The Tibetan system uses five basic chakras. The spinning of the chakras and the speed at which they spin will determine the vitality and vibrant health of each chakra and the body. The chakras affect the vitality of the endocrine system and all the organs, creating healing, magnetism, and rejuvenation. In the Kabbalah, there are four main levels of ten major sefirot in each level. Sefira means 'counting' and pertains to centres.

Gradually practice noticing the subtle energies. As you learn to listen to and feel the flow of energy, you will be able to master it almost at will. Martial arts masters can 'think' their energy to a limb or an organ. They use their willpower to direct the energy. It is a mastery of mind over matter, concentrating the energy.

This amazing vehicle, the temple of your soul, is your divine human body. The following simple practice will transform your health and your sense of well-being. It will also transform the way you perceive the world and people throughout the day. You, the giver, can bathe the receiver in your mind's eye in gold and silver light. Invite him or her to breathe gold and silver into his or her being. Internally, call him or her by name. You may visualize, feel, taste, or hear the experience.

We all have different ways of perceiving the world. Some people are predominantly kinaesthetic and tactile; they can feel what the sense gives them. Touch and feelings are their doorway to access their being. Touch is the way they interpret the world. If you invite a kinaesthetic person to focus on a sense of fruit in his or her hand, he or she may report feeling the texture or the weight of that fruit.

Some people are predominantly visual and perceive the world in pictures. They can see the colours, shapes, and lighting. They can easily conjure up an image in their mind's eye and could construct images. A few people can even detect with their naked eye infrared and ultraviolet colours, which are on both ends of the rainbow colour spectrum.

Some individuals experience by taste, some by smell. They are predominantly olfactory. Many chefs and perfumers are gifted with this ability. Some individuals are fortunate to be able to taste colour; this is called neurological synaesthesia. An auditory person would perceive the world predominantly through sound and have the gift of being sensitive to sounds, music, even the sounds of the universe and words. They possess an acute sense of hearing. The spoken word or music can ignite their imagination and could turn them on, and they have the tendency to be great thinkers or musicians. Some individuals are gifted with a clear all pervasive 'knowing'. Others use any combination of these sensory tools. When interacting with others, listen and pay attention to the language they use to describe things. This will give you clues as to what sense is predominating.

Working with tantric meditations and with other tools described in this book, will help you to balance and open up to the possibilities of the other senses. When a memory is triggered, the other senses will be switched on and activated. In the case of a trauma release, they may shut down and close in response. The more you work consciously with the senses, the more you will be able to tune into and detect sensitive subtle energies.

Practice

Cultivating the Taoist practice of the 'inner smile' is a superb daily health promotion. In the morning, take few moments to focus your attention without being distracted by external stimuli. Simply go inwards with your attention and deliberately scan through your body and organs.

Start from the base chakra in the perineum, between the anus and the genitals. Travel with your awareness and intention all the way up to the crown chakra at the top of your head. The key is to smile at your organs, limbs, and being. This may take a few seconds, or you can indulge in longer meditation, enjoying the calmness that permeates through your whole being as you cultivate this profound yet simple self-healing practice.

THE CHAKRA MODELS

The images used here follow the Hindu tradition.

First Chakra, Muladhara

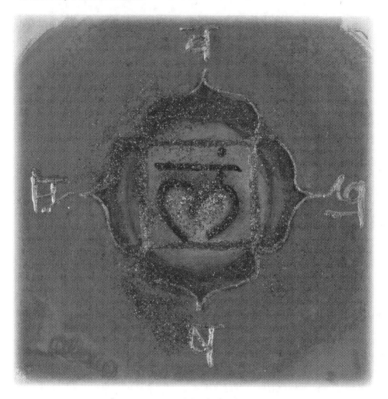

Image 08: First Chakra, *Muladhara*

The first chakra is known as the base or root chakra or *muladhara*. It is situated at the perineum and is associated with the colour red. It is regarded as a masculine, positive chakra. In the male, this area of the body (the genitals) is more pronounced and protrudes, whereas in the female it is receptive and is hidden. This chakra centre is concerned with the basic love of life; it is the seat of our passion and the source of our kundalini energy, our life-force energy. It is the position of our root to the earth; it grounds us and embodies the quality of support.

This chakra is associated with the sense of smell, the sexual glands, and the endocrine glands. It is about our ability to contain and experience ecstasy and orgasmic qualities which are also experiencing abundance.

Each chakra has a *bija*, a seed or single syllable sound; the base chakra seed sounds are *lang, sam, sham,* and *vam.* This chakra is represented by the elephant god Ganesh and is depicted by a square shape. A clear and healthy base chakra is fundamentally important, as it is the foundation for all other developments. It is concerned with our need for security and assurance. It is also related to our basic needs and functions, such as food, sex, health, and excretion. It is involved with generating more passion to fuel and propel energy upwards to power the upper chakras for enlightenment. It relates to the *malchut sefira*, kingdom centre, manifestation on earth, in the Kabbalist system.

Second Chakra, Swadhisthana

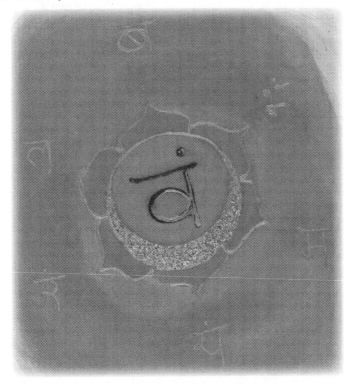

41

Image 09: Second Chakra, *Swadhisthana*

The second chakra, known as the sacral centre, is called *svadhisthana* or *swadhisthana* chakra. It is situated around the internal reproductive organs and abdomen below the navel. Orange is the associated colour. This chakra is usually regarded as a feminine positive chakra, as it has the capacity to grow when carrying a child. It is the point of our source and origin.

It represents stability and is where our balance centre, the *hara* or *dan-tien* is located. Known as the energy command centre, the second chakra is the centre of creativity, the seat of emotions and our fluidity of being. It is our energetic umbilical cord connection to our mother and our ancestry. It is associated with the element of water and the sense of taste. The second chakra is also associated with adrenal glands and our fluidity, vitality, health, balance, and ease in our being.

The seed syllables for the second chakra mantra are *wang, vang, bam, bham, nam, yam, ram,* or *lam.* It is represented by the mythical 'makara' – half-alligator, half-fish, and depicted as a half moon. In the Kabbalistic tradition this chakra is related to the *yesod sefira*, the foundation. It is the source of *kriya shakti* – action energy for breaking through blockages.

Third Chakra, **Manipura**

Image 10: Third Chakra, *Manipura*

The third chakra is known as the solar plexus or *manipura*. Traditionally, this chakra is located around the navel. In the new-age schools of spirituality, it is said to be situated more towards the sternum. This varies according to the individual; for practical purposes it may be found anywhere between these two positions.

This chakra is associated with the colour yellow. It is regarded as a masculine positive chakra; it represents the masculine quality of willpower. The essential balancing and harmonizing quality of this chakra is playfulness. It is associated with the element of fire and the sense of sight. It is where the joy of the soul resides.

The third chakra is related to the pancreas, our self-esteem, charisma, willpower, playfulness, radiance, and how we manifest in the world. The seed syllable for the third chakra is rang. It is represented by the image of the ram, denoting controlled anger, and by a downwards pointing triangle. This chakra is also regarded as the umbilical cord to the universal soul, manifesting the energy that is needed by humanity to feel goodness and harmony within and the ability to feel empathy towards the environment and others.

On either side of the third chakra are two sub-chakras, located by the last ribs.

Hidden Secret Chakra, Hrit Chakra

Image 11: Hidden Secret Chakra, *Hrit Chakra*

The secret chakra or hrit chakra, is nestled just below the heart chakra, and is used in the Shakta tradition of tantra. It is represented by eight petals of white, gold, or red colour. It is depicted by the image of a vacant seat under a bodhi tree, illustrating the message that it is only when your inner guru appears that you are awakened. The most distinctive quality of this chakra is the mythical bodhi tree, depicted in the centre of the image.

It is said that the Yogi rests under the bodhi tree at the end of his journey, when the Buddha appears there all by himself, which is the blessing!

It is also referred to as sat guru chakra, the true teacher centre.

Fourth Chakra, Anahata

Image 12: Fourth Chakra, *Anahata*

The fourth chakra is known as the heart chakra, or *anahata*. It is located in the centre of the chest. It is associated with the colours green and pink. This heart chakra is regarded as positive for females and receptive for males.

The qualities for this chakra are unconditional love, acceptance, equanimity, and true compassion. It is also associated with psychological balance. The forth chakra is associated with the thymus glands, the desire to merge with all that is, innocence, empathy, and compassion.

The seed syllable for the fourth chakra is *yang* or *young* (at heart). It is sometimes represented by a star with a gold triangle and a linga (phallic symbol) in union with female yoni, the source of all. Other times it may be represented by twelve petals of a red or white hue, with the centre part a smoky colour. It is the midpoint of the upper and lower chakras and is associated with the mixing of the white and red energies of heaven and earth. It is associated with the air *tattva* element. It is the *jivatman*, the seat of the divine soul, our higher self. It is the energy of emotional expression, the ability to love and create harmony, the unstruck sound, an eternal continual sound in the heart.

There are also two more sub-chakras, either on each side of the breast or on the nipple. This can vary from person to person.

Fifth Chakra, **Vishuddha**

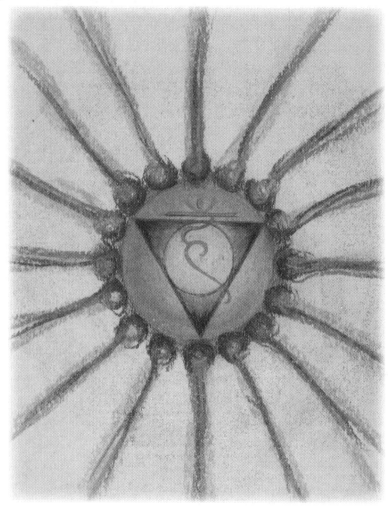

Image 13: Fifth Chakra, *Vishuddha*

The throat chakra, *vishuddha chakra*, is connected to speaking the truth, healing the masculine aspects, and changing karma. It is the male positive chakra and is receptive in females. It represents purity, clarity, and truth. It is depicted by a circle, and its seed syllable is *hang*. The colour is blue. The throat chakra is associated with the thyroid glands and our ability to assert ourselves in authentic expression and inspire others with our truth.

Traditionally, the chakra is depicted by a white elephant and represents the support that brings spiritual fulfilment. It is the centre for spiritual expression and objective view. It is the seat of karma, cause and effect in tantra kriya yoga. It is also where the father and masculine issues reside.

In shakta tantra it is represented by sixteen smoke-coloured petals, each linked with one of the Sanskrit vowels. The centre colour is white, transparent, smoke, or sky-blue. It is associated with *akasha*, the space element, where our connection and ability to transmit and channel universal knowledge and truth are connected.

Sixth Chakra, the Third Eye – Ajna

Image 14: Sixth Chakra, the Third Eye – *Ajna*

The third eye, the sixth chakra, *ajna* is traditionally regarded as the feminine positive chakra, though the secret male aspect of this chakra is in the occiput, the *medulla oblongata*, where the spine enters the skull. This chakra is regarded in the new-age schools as the intuition centre, though not in the original tantric texts, where traditionally it is the seat of wisdom, consciousness, and awareness. It is representing the formless spaciousness. It is associated with the pituitary glands.

The seed syllable mantra is *ang* or *tzang*. It is the command centre of the guru – the bringer of enlightenment or spiritual guide, or a modern day guru, such as a psychotherapist, shedding light on things. The chakra is located in between the eyebrows. It is represented by two petals and the shape of the full moon. It is associated with the *manas* or mind *tattva*. The image is white in colour. It is Shakti and Shiva in union, the god and goddess Hakni Shakti. The qualities are grace and respect. The colour of the chakra in the body is purple or violet. It is about the ability to 'see' and connect to the collective unconsciousness, the universal wisdom. This chakra is responsible for balancing and harmonizing the time and space continuum.

Some new-age schools regard the mind and the ego as a hindrance and advocate for their dissolution, while some call to 'slay' the ego, claiming that it is not helpful for our spiritual evolution. If fact, as we strengthen our 'spiritual muscles', we stretch our super ego. The ego is the bridge to the self. You need to strengthen it in order to let it go, which is a paradox. The ego helps us function in life.

To assist in understanding the beneficial aspects of the ego, it will be helpful to look at the work of Ken Wilber. There are three broad realms in Ken Wilber's modality:

1. The **pre-personal is** where most conventional therapy aims to produce a functioning adult in the world.

2. The **personal** extends that to become a fuller, broader human being, including emotions, creativity, and the spirit.

3. The **transpersonal**, is the realm of spiritual practices aiming to allow the realisation of oneness with the divine or unity consciousness.

Each person will experience each of these states in varying degrees during the day, depending on their emotional states as they experience life. The West, with its winning blend of consumerism and individualism, turns everything into a form of therapy and ultimately a narcissistic enterprise, as it has with yoga and now with tantra.

Tantra is a spiritual path, but again from Wilber, spirituality means different things for people who are at different stages of consciousness. In India much tantra was and probably still is primarily at the level of superstition, offering protection from 'evil' and help to gain advantage. For this reason, as well as the residue of India's long history of puritan occupation, tantrics in India today are synonymous with black magic and death and are considered very unsavoury characters. Spiritual practice, particularly if it includes the body, is a preparation for death, and this further increases suspicion. For any letting go is a death of the small self with which we can easily identify.

Ego is in the realm of pre-personal and personal development in Ken Wilber's model of human spiritual evolution. The self, or dissolution to all that is, is in the realm of the transpersonal, where tantra is positioned alongside Christianity, Buddhism, Judaism, etc. – all teachings that are calling for unity consciousness. Sadly, many do not live up to the ideal of their religions.

We have different roles on the levels of personality, like the clothes we wear. They are how we tend to identify ourselves, but they can change with time and circumstance. They mask our vulnerabilities layer, consciously or not. Behind these layers lies our true essence, our divinity, where the Buddha, Allah, Elohim, the Shchina or Shakina, or the Christ within resides. This is who we really are, beyond personalities and stories and identification with thoughts, events, or possessions. Our true essence, our light, is always there; we just need to remember to allow ourselves to see and reconnect with our light and the connection to all that is.

It is through bringing awareness and consciousness that we dissolve the ego. Awareness is the platform upon which all life plays its fascinating games. The dance of Shakti (the goddess, feminine) is on the platform of Shiva (the god, masculine).

The Palatine Chakras

Image 15: The Palatine Chakras

It is the *talu* or *lalana* centre in shakta tantra. In Taoism it is referred to as the 'heavenly pool'. There are three sub-chakras located along the soft palate on the roof of the mouth. These are activated via the tongue acting as a master switch.

Guru Chakra

Image 16: Guru Chakra

The guru chakra is a sub-chakra to the seventh, the crown chakra. It is located between the *nirvana* (lower) and *sahasrara* (higher) crown chakras. The nirvana is the supreme godhead or the *bodhini*, the awakened consciousness chakra. In Tibetan Buddhism it is called *swabhavakaya*, absolute self-nature. In Taoism it is referred to as the 'one hundred meetings' – *bai hui*, Kun Lun Mountain (the highest peak of heaven).

It is connected to spiritual dimensions and planes of consciousness beyond and above the separate individual self. It is the place where we receive spiritual and intellectual revelations from higher planes of existence. It is in the cave of brahma, the space inside the brain associated with the pineal gland.

It is also known as the *brahmarandha* chakra. At death, the spirit leaves the body through a tiny hole at the top of the head.

It is activated when you are genuinely in touch with your own inner guru. The hidden guru chakra is also referred as the 'fourth eye'. It is said that those born with a mark on the fourth eye have special insights and are called *maha kali* (female) or *maha kala* (male).

Seventh Chakra, Sahasrara, Nirvana - Parabrahma *Chakra*

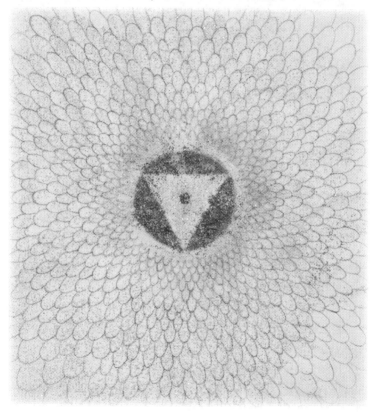

Image 17: Seventh Chakra, *Sahasrara, Nirvana, Parabrahma* Chakra

This the crown chakra. Different traditions vary as to whether the *sahasrara* chakra, or 'thousand-petalled lotus', is located at the crown point at the very top of the head or above the head. The petals are arranged in twenty layers each made up from fifty petals. The word *sahasrara* is often described as meaning 'a thousand petals'. However, this is a mistranslation; *sahasrara* is more accurately translated as 'a lot'.

Its colour is white, sometimes with a violet hue, sometimes silver or transparent, shining brighter than the full moon. It is formless and senseless, which is beyond the ordinary perception using the five gross senses of touch, smell, taste, sight, and sound.

It represents unity or union. The sound symbols in the chakras are the sound energy of the kundalini – sexual life force energy as it rises. The crown chakra's sound, *om* or *aum*, is the sound of the universe, the sum of all sounds. The crown is beyond the duality of separation; it is our connection to all that is. It is where divinity/spirit/light enter us.

The crown chakra symbolizes detachment from illusion, which is essential in achieving higher/pure consciousness and realization of the truth that all is one. The crown chakra is associated with the pineal gland, transcendence being the bridge between heaven and earth.

All other chakras emanate from the crown. Immortality is the quality of this chakra. *Samadhi* is the bliss state that a yogi achieves when sexual kundalini energy rises up to his crown. Relating to the pineal gland that helps with shamanic journeys and visions, it is also called *brahma-randhra*, the meeting place of Shakti kundalini and Shiva consciousness. It is the marriage of the opposites.

Shri Yantra, Nava *chakra*

Image 18: *Shri Yantra*

The highest tantric symbol is depicting the union of the feminine and masculine principles and the source of all existence at the centre point, the *bindu*. It is the symbol of the wisdom goddess Tripura Sundari, the goddess of the three realms, also known as Lalitha. Meditating on the *shri yantra*, the holly wheel or divine instrument, can help us to self-realize.

The *shri yantra* is comprised of nine interlocking triangles that emanate from the *bindu*, the meeting place of the manifest world of phenomena, physical realm and the unmanifested full potentiality. The five large downward-pointing triangles represent Shakti, the feminine aspects. The large four upward-pointing triangles represent Shiva, the masculine aspects.

The weaving of the nine (*nava*) large triangles creates forty-three smaller triangles representing the whole yoniverse, the cosmic womb. It is the symbol of the *advaita* tantra, the non-dual path of oneness. It is also one of the symbols for the eighth chakra, the energy bodies. The nine worlds represent the wisdom goddesses.

CHAKRA TABLE

The basic chakras may be translated into the following simple messages in relation to the self and others.

Base (first chakra)	I need.	I notice you; I give.
Belly (second chakra)	I want and desire.	I desire to connect with you.
Navel/solar (third chakra)	I share and play.	I offer my power and playfulness in sharing.
Hrit (secret chakra)	I devote and surrender.	I feel you deeply; I receive.
Heart (fourth chakra)	I accept.	I accept you unconditionally.
Throat (fifth chakra)	I am changing karma.	I hear you and your truth; together we are instrumental to change.
Palatine (secret inner mastery chakras)	I express truth.	I offer my truth to you.
Third eye (sixth chakra)	I see your beauty.	I see you as you really are and your potential beyond my projections.
Guru chakra (hidden guru chakra, the fourth eye)	I am open to receiving bliss and Shakti-pat transmissions.	I share our collective wisdom and transmissions.
Crown (seventh chakra)	I am.	I am you; we are one.

SHUSHUMNA

The central channel within the body is called *Shushumna*. It is like the underground metro or the subway trains stations. Each chakra is like a station. The chakras could be also represented by a three-dimensional image of American footballs overlapping.

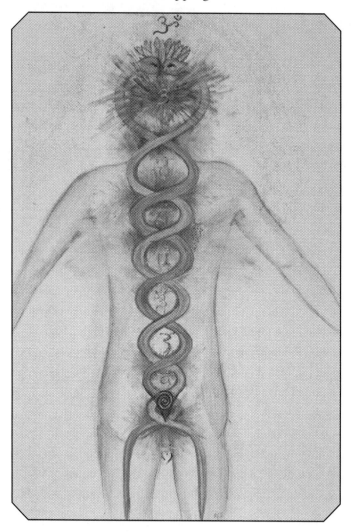

Image 20: *Shushumna*

Kabbalist Ten Sefirot

The Kabbalah is the Jewish tantra; it is the basis for Jewish and Christian mysticism. It uses ten sefirot (energy centres, meaning counting). These are the Kabbalist chakras, which are also doorways to the four levels of being, manifestation, and consciousness:

1. emanation (*atzilut*)

2. creation (*briyah*)

3. formation (*yetzira*)

4. action (*asiyah*)

Bridging each level are the ten sefirot, providing the portals by which the human spirit forms the link between heaven and earth. The light in the Kabbalah or *zimzumim*, the divine essence, enters via the crown (*keter*), zigzagging through the sefirot, the chakras, and manifesting on earth through the kingdom chakra at the base, at the root.

The Tree of Life – Sefirot

Divine light / Existence

Ruach Elohit / Ha Or / Ha Yekum

Zimzumim / Divinity zigzags in,
Divine essence, the Light enters and though the Keter/crown, all
the way down to manifest on earth through the:

0. *Crown*

Keter כֶּתֶר

1. *Understanding*	2. *Wisdom*
Binah בִּינָה	Chochmah חָכְמָה

3. *Knowledge*

Da'at דַּעַת

4. *Might / Bravery*	5. *Loving Kindness*
Gevurah גְּבוּרָה	Chesed חֶסֶד

6. *Beauty / Splendor*

Tiferet תִּפְאֶרֶת

7.5 *The Secret Sfira*
Hrit / Neshama
The Shchina Penetrated / The Dwelling Place of the
Shchina/ The Way Through Chadra חָדְרָ(ה) / Hadar הדר

7. *Acknowledgment /*	8 *Victory / Eternity*
Grace Hod הוֹד	Netzach נֶצַח

9 *Foundation / Origins*
Yesod יְסוֹד

10 *Kingdom / Manifest on Earth*
Malchut מַלְכוּת

Image 20a: Kabbalist Sefirot

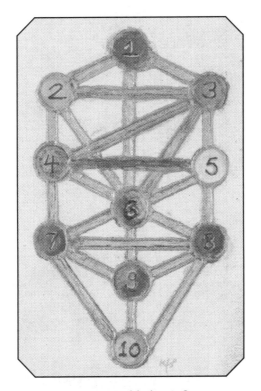

Image 21: Kabbalist Sefirot

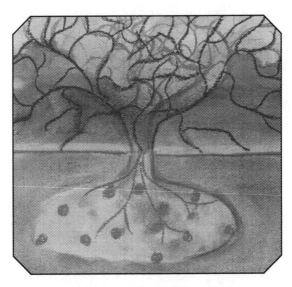

Image 22: Kabbalist Tree of Life

CHAPTER 7:

Mantras, Divine Music

Aum

Is the universal sound,

The sound of the Universe/Yoniverse.

SOME ANCIENT SANSKRIT TEXTS say there is no tantra without mantra!

Mantras are sacred sounds that activate energy and consciousness within the body. The use of mantras, chants, or affirmations is a vital ingredient in tantra. They can be in any language. Traditional mantras and blessings were in Aramaic, Arabic, Hebrew, Sanskrit, and Latin. 'Man-' means 'mind' and '-tra' means 'quiet'.

'Yoni' means the sacred place of all or the source of all, pertaining to the vulva. Through tantric meditations, you can experience the whole universe opening up in the woman's yoni.

Mantra can help create change in the lives of the person chanting or receiving. You chant as an honouring to the god or the goddess lying in front of you, while you massage them. The intention is honouring and devotional service. It is one of the most important elements of the ritual.

Working with honouring chants, mantras, and affirmations is one of the secrets for a successful tantric massage. Having music playing in the background is great, but chanting yourself makes it tantric. It is the devotional embodiment and expression of the mantra that constitute the magic.

Embodying a mantra or affirmation is an important part of a daily tantric practice. You can chant, sing, or whisper either in your language or in the ancient sacred languages. Sanskrit is said to be the sacred language of the gods, not spoken as everyday speech. It is not an everyday language. There are fifty letters in the Sanskrit alphabet. Each syllable can mean many different things depending on context and the placing in a mantra and can resonate in different parts of the body.

The sounds have energetic resonance, and they affect our energy and our physicality. When you chant while honouring your partner, you penetrate the core of their being without them needing to understand the meaning of the words; they receive the transmission of the energy.

A genuine committed tantric practitioner will be chanting or singing the mantra throughout the whole massage, apart from the time they are guiding the receiver deeper. It is a prayer; it is devotional.

Testimonial

> To hear the women chanting while attending to the men was so deep I was transported far away, maybe to Aztec or Indian tribe culture. (R.)

Mantras are transcendental sounds, producing specific responses in the physical body. The power is in the sound, not the meaning of the word, though the meaning is loaded with potent creative power. These sounds and chants can be whispered, sung, meditated, celebrated, and integrated to allow their blessings to permeate our lives. Chanting the mantras will result in creating more love, joy, abundance, and healing. Using mantras consciously will bring resolution to ailments and afflictions and will produce karma.

The creative power is in the sound. Most are ancient chants, songs, and mantras from all over the world and from various cultures. They resonate in our bodies, uplift our spirit, and liberate our souls. Nowadays it is possible to measure sound vibration. Sound affects everything, and everything has vibration. Every cell is vibrating at a frequency; even urine and blood have a vibration and a sound they emit.

Repeating a mantra will enable us to tune inwards, becoming still in our minds, which leads to a growing awareness of the subtle energies around. Mantras cultivate serenity. Mantras can start audibly. A mantra can last for a short duration of a few minutes or for hours, days, months, or years. A subsequent sense of completion will be felt at some point. Mantras create a healing vibration that resonates in the body, mind, and soul.

Another way to use a chant mantra is to vocalize the mantra on exhalation, creating a vibration that originates in the physical body. On inhalation, internalize the mantra. The silent mantra will reverberate in the etheric body. The sound mantra on exhalation awakens and uses the Shakti-kundalini energy, our latent raw sexual life force energy, manifesting in etheric resonance, realizing the power of the chakra.

The chakra system corresponds to the organs in the body – the heart, lungs etc. As you have not physically seen your heart but you trust in your mind and body that it is there, so is your heart chakra. Consciously imagining the flow of energy will result in becoming receptive to these energies.

Experiment with the mantras; see what they invoke in you. Whatever the emotion – be it anger, joy, sadness, or bliss – tantra welcomes all expressions of our being.

Pronunciation is both very important and not important at all. On the one hand, pronunciation is so important, because uttering the sacred sounds could bring healing, break down barriers, and perhaps blast cancerous cells. That is why teaching by an accomplished practitioner or guru is important. On the other hand, the intention itself contributes to the beneficial 'magical' effects. One of my mantra teachers said that the sound that emanates from within is the right one for us. It is said that the Buddha gave a poor woman a mantra which she mispronounced constantly for many days. However, her intention and conviction was so pure and she was so focused on her task that it had the desired effect. Relax and enjoy making mistakes.

Laughter is also very healing. The Dalai Lama frequently laughs. Spirituality does not have to mean seriousness and sombreness. This practice cultivates healing, health, and wellbeing.

Here are some chants to give you a taste from my book *Sacred Chants and Mantras* due for publication later this year.

PRACTICE

On exhalation, express the mantra clearly and steadily. Gradually decrease the volume of the mantra until you internalize it, hearing it in your mind (and in the body as well). When a sound vibration is internalized, resonating within, it generates power.

I Am Tranquillity

Aum Shanti

The meaning of this chant is 'I am tranquillity; I am the light; I am peace.'

The chant can be whispered, sung in different tunes, or chanted. You could even make your own tune or 'borrow' another tune that you feel affinity with.

Abundance Goddess Mantra

Aum Shrim Maha, Lakshmiyei Swaha

This mantra is for affluence, prosperity and abundance mantra to the goddess Lakshmi.

The syllable *aum* is commonly voiced as a prefix to mantras of all kinds, because it is the seed sound for the sixth chakra, where masculine and feminine energies meet at the centre of the brow.

Shrim is the seed sound for the principle of abundance. Repetition of the *shrim* mantra gives one the ability to attract and maintain abundance.

Maha means 'great', in context denoting both quantity and quality. When we speak of the quality of abundance here, we are referring to its harmony with divine law.

Lakshmi in Sanskrit means 'the energy of abundance'. Abundance is usually thought of as simple prosperity.

Swaha means 'I surrender to my true nature to divinity' or 'Halleluiah'.

Kabbalist Mantra

Yud Hei Vav Hei

The name of God. The breath of life and light. Opening of the portal of the Vault of the Adepts. These are the letters of the sacred name of God, Jehovah in Hebrew. Breathing the name of God, remembering your divine nature, surrendering to who you really are and allowing existence to permeate your whole being.

Union Mantra

Aum Ahadi Aum

All is one. All is divine, the sacred and the mundane, the genitals and the crown. Every activity is sacred – from praying to self-pleasuring, to urinating, and to defecating. All is part of the divine. There is a sequence to follow while touching the body and chanting. To obtain a copy of this practice, please contact http://www.tantra.uk.com.

Beyond the Beyond

Gate Gate, Para Gate, Para Sum Gate, Bodhi Swaha

The meaning of this mantra is 'Beyond the beyond, even further then the beyond, even further than that, Oh Awakened One (you), I salute and surrender to you. Halleluiah.'

Universal Peace

Sh – Aha – L – Aum

Sh is the universal sound representing silence. *Aha* opens the heart. *L* activates the pineal gland and serotonin. *Aum* is the sound of the whole universe.

This mantra is to be chanted over one breath length. Shalom means 'peace' and is a greeting in Hebrew.

CHAPTER 8:

Kundalini

THE SACRUM IS THE seat of the kundalini, the latent raw sexual energy, depicted as a snake coiled in the sacrum, creating more power, energy, and consciousness, as it is rising up the spine. It is our raw life-force energy.

Activating the kundalini will bring empowerment, clarity, and connection to universal consciousness. Kundalini could be experienced as a hot sensation rising and a tranquil trickle of blissful nectar or a technicolour light show. Kundalini is the most powerful and profound manifestation of the raw sexual energy, yet it is so easily accessible to all.

We direct the raw sexual energy to transmute and transform it into a creative expression of love or to release the manifesting power of a project we wish to accomplish.

The emphasis in tantric healing massage is on stimulating and awakening, guiding and directing, nurturing and honouring the flow of energy around and in your partner's body. The anterior spot on the coccyx bone is the kunda point. This is the end of the kundalini tail when it is dormant. When it is awakened, it will feel hot, as if it is being ignited. Sometimes it can be experienced like a match stick being flared up. This is often the description when kundalini is awakened. While massaging the back to activate the kundalini, it is best to keep the head in a straight line with the spine. This will enable the kundalini to rise up the spine into the *medulla oblongata.*

Many books have been written warning people of the dangers of the awakened kundalini and its activation. Some of this is due to fear of the uncontrollable power that could be unleashed. Some of the reasons are to have power and control over people. It is highly potent, and you should be very respectful of its latent power. That is why it is symbolized as the snake, and the most profound practices are from the tantra *kriya yoga*, the cosmic cobra breath. The cobra is the king of the snakes.

There are practices you can cultivate to endure the safe release of this potent power. Learning to ride this powerful phenomenon is like learning to ride a surf board, as you will never be able to control the waves. It is very important to find an acknowledged or accomplished practitioner or known teachers to help with your initiation in these practices. The tantric practices described here are safe to use, though if you are susceptible to any of the health warnings described in the front of the book, please seek professional advice. To harness safely this powerful

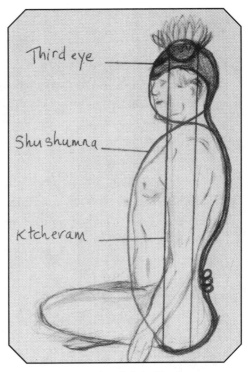

Image 23: Kundalini Shushumna

kundalini energy, it would be highly advisable to be initiated in the cobra breath practices of the tantra *kriya yoga*. You can find out more on http://www.tantra.uk.com/tky

CHAPTER 9: NUDITY AND
SEXUAL EXPRESSION

TANTRIC MASSAGE IS OFTEN received naked; the more exposed skin there is, the more the whole body is integrated and included.

Testimonial

A hidden energy was coming out … something deep within that I have been trying to contact or connect with for quite some time. Thank you for allowing me to fully engage with that 'part' of being. It took me back, and I still feel as I am integrating it. (E.D.)

It was so natural and simple yet so profound. Being naked was the most liberating experience after the religious indoctrination. Thank you. I was touched by God in my heart and every cell of my body. (G.I.)

The giver does not need to be in the nude, though with love partners it is often the case, and it is beautiful to witness and receive the arousal of a partner. If the man is giving a massage and he is affected by his beloved being highly aroused, they can both enjoy his erection without needing to do anything about the erection; it is just a sign that the giver is also affected and enjoying the process. As the giver, you can also be naked with your lover. Then there is no difference, no separation, and no hierarchy.

This may not be appropriate in the case of clients, as some boundaries are important to establish and maintain. It is vitally important to respect the contracts and agreements made prior to the session, particularly with clients, as changing the goal posts or the boundaries will be unsafe for the receiver, even though they may desire this during the massage. If an agreement was verbalized that the genitals will not be included during the massage and a man is receiving, it is important to respect this, even if he may feel aroused and wishes to enjoy this. Changing the agreement will not serve either of you.

What could occur during the massage as the receiver is lying down is that they may regress and become vulnerable. In this case, the way most people reach out is through the sexual arousal, and often they override their true needs in favour of an instant gratification. Alternatively, it may be an attempt to try to please the therapist or partner, depending on what is happening in the couple's dynamics or the unconscious projections of a client.

There is a lot of misunderstanding about what tantric massage is, and some people use it as a titillating marketing tool. It is neither a new-age 'hand job' nor a form of sexual relief. This misperception, of course, is due to the plethora of sex workers rebranding themselves as tantric goddesses and *dakas* or *dakinis*. The misuse of the title by individuals who may be damaged emotionally and sexually has contributed to the misconceptions about tantra and tantric massage. It is for this reason that I reiterate the emphasis on healing and integrity throughout my teachings and practice, in order to differentiate myself from those who may be misusing the title.

Due to the sensitive nature of this work, social misunderstanding, dogmas, and judgments, most clients prefer to keep the nature of the session confidential. People around the world love to have me as their best-kept secret.

It is imperative that the practitioner is self-aware and has solid daily tantric practices and knowledge of tantra. A tantric practitioner has an immense duty of care. When it comes to working with sexual energy, an honest discussion is immeasurably valuable. It is healthy and mature to have a discussion about sexuality and sexual health history, discussing the outcomes, hopes, and expectations of both giver and receiver. Some people go into a fantasy inside their heads and do not connect to reality. There is nothing more exquisite then a real live god or goddess being massaged by a worshiping and honouring partner.

For a male practitioner giving to a female client, I would highly advise being at least partially clothed with trousers. This will be respectful and will enable the woman to feel trusting and safe. If a client has been abused, the unconscious wish to re-enact the abuse is a futile attempt at resolving it and could repeat the abuse story in their perception.

Often male clients wish to have the female practitioner nude. This may be due to their need to see and feel the nakedness of the female body in close proximity. Some men may be unconfident about a women's body. Some clients are starved of intimacy in long-term relationships where partners are taken for granted or are in sexless relationships.

Men are different from women of course, and so the intentions and purpose of the tantric healing massage may be vastly different. For some men it may be just a simple need to have an erotic expression in a safe environment that does not violate their marital commitments. Tantra works with the polarities of feminine and masculine within each person. Therefore, in same gender couples, one partner can embody more of one polarity and so can be the giver in the massage; the receiver will embody the opposite polarity. The massage can balance and complement naturally, harmonizing the inner masculine and feminine.

Heterosexual and bisexual men may have a greater need to look at and adore the beautiful naked body of a goddess than a woman does. It is said in ancient tantric texts that a man can achieve enlightenment by simply meditating on the naked body of the goddess, and specifically on her yoni, the sacred vulva, the source of all. Some men need to heal old wounds from rejections and lack of touch or fear of the female body. Sometimes it is appropriate for the woman practitioner to place the client's hand on her thigh or arm or even breasts. This is to be determined by the goddess herself, providing she is clear and has worked through her own male relationship issues and sexuality. Exercising appropriateness is paramount.

It is vitally important that the practitioners are sexually fulfilled in their own lives so that there will be no need to act from desire when arousal occurs during a session. To achieve this, the practitioner needs to engage regularly in nourishing and nurturing their own sexuality and fulfilling their own sexual needs, either through sacred sexual union that helps transmute sexual energy or by self-pleasuring and dedication, honouring their vital life force energy. Thus they will be comfortable in their own sexuality as it may arise and will not feel compelled to act upon it.

Testimonial

Such a holistic experience indeed! And this does not go for the 'body and soul massage' only but also for the conversation we had before and after the massage. I will keep our discussion and your advice as a life guide – a life where loving and caring is of utmost importance. You managed to understand my needs and addressed those from our first meeting. I already experience the reframing of sex into something of higher and divine at a personal level but most importantly to my relation with my wife. (M.I.T.M.)

BODY SLIDE

Body slide is wonderful to share with your lover and can be highly arousing for both partners, as well as emotionally nourishing. It is also called body-to-body. Some practitioners offer this practice. Be mindful, as you are merging your energies in a more visceral way, and your emotional bodies as well.

As a practitioner, you are invited to embody respect to the divine temple which is the body. As you are teaching and transmitting it to others, you also have a 'duty of care' to yourself, to embody self-respect and self-honouring.

Chapter 10:

Breath, Sound, and Movement

THE BASIC FIRST THREE keys in tantra, and the most important keys to tantra and tantric healing massage, are breath, sound, and movement. Make sure you use these at all times. Return to the breath, sound, and movement to facilitate deeper relaxation. The giver can remind the receiver of these keys by using their own audible exhalation during the massage. This will help the receiver to drop to a deeper level.

Breath, sound, and movement will help you anchor the experience in your body. They are the keys that will help you integrate the energies and will also enable you to move through whatever is arising into a state that is higher and more blissful, touching grace itself. As the giver, you will need to embody comfort in your own body. You will transmit and communicate comfort to your beloved. As you exhale out loudly, the receiver will be reminded to exhale. When they exhale, they will be able to let go even more into a state of receptivity and surrender.

Using the exhalation is a safety release valve, like in a pressure cooker. The exhalation will facilitate easy transformation and transition in awareness, physically and emotionally. Exhaling consciously will ensure you are having an easier ride in the rollercoaster of life and experiences.

BREATH

This is the tantric number one basic key used in tantra and any transformation work. When we are in fear, we tend to hold the breath. In yoga, breathing techniques are called *pranayama*. *Prana* is life-force energy, and *yama* means to extend/control, and so *pranayama* means 'extension of the life force'. *Yama* also has the meaning of 'death'.

The word 'inhale' or 'inspire' is derived from the word *in-spiritus* in Latin, meaning 'god within', taking divinity into you. 'Exhale' or 'expire' means 'letting go' or 'death', surrendering to all that we are. Every breath we take is a new moment, a new life. Every exhalation we let go, is a letting go and surrendering into what is, into the moment. The more we exhale, the more we let go, the more we let go, the more new can come in, as we have made space in our being. The more you let go, the more you can contain.

The slower you breathe, the longer you live. Slow breathing mammals, such as tortoises and whales, breathe slowly and live longer than small animals such as birds and mice.

In tantra yoga we are aware of the breath, as it is the carrier of transformation. Some say we have a finite number of breaths in a lifetime, so the slower you breathe the longer you live. You can reduce stress and enjoy longer life, health, and vitality if you practice conscious breathing.

SOUND

Sound is the fastest vehicle of transformation in tantra yoga. You will benefit by making sounds for healing to occur in the throat chakra, changing karma and opening the heart chakra.

It is vital that the receiver should be encouraged to release sound during the massage. This will help provide clues to the masseur as to whether it is enjoyable or painful. Making the sound 'ahh' is important; as you let go of the sound, you also exhale. The more you let go, the more new can come in. The sound 'ahh' opens the heart centre, the heart chakra. The use of mantras has already been touched upon in this book, but real understanding will come from integration into the practice. Work with mantras that you chant rather than only playing music in the background. Sing along with it. Work with one mantra for a while, and you will see its effect on your being.

It is said that sound is the fastest path to enlightenment. *Nada* yoga, the yoga of sound, uses mantras and seed syllables, just as the *shofar*, the Jewish ram horn, is used to announce the arrival of the New Year. The conch or other tantric instruments are used to announce tantric indigenous practices and rituals. In the Old Testament there is the story of the walls of Jericho tumbling down from the sound of the *shofar*. Opera singers can shatter glass with their voice. Sound is a vibration that carries through all matter, solid, liquid and air. As the human body is approximately 75 per cent water, it conducts sound and enables the resonance to reverberate and have miraculous effects on the body. It may be that we evolved from the sea; we 'brought' the sea within us.

There is a yoga practice called *yoni mudra*, the gesture of the tomb, where we seal all facial orifices and use alternate nose breathing. After twenty minutes you can hear the sound of life and the blood 'mantra', the compassion mantra or the royal liberation *mukti* mantra, the *so ham*. It sounds like the sounds of the sea. When people think they may have a blockage in their body or their chakras, they can blast it with a sound that will help dissolve the energetic holding. You may be aware of the effect classical music has on plants.

MOVEMENT

Movement is a vital ingredient in a tantric healing massage. The practitioner needs to be fluid and dance around the body, flowing, rotating, and swaying with the energy that is generated. You will need to encourage the recipient to dance and flow as if they are a snake. Encourage them to take charge, to claim and amplify their sexual energy. This will also enhance the sexual arousal and change the way they relate to being aroused. Tantra means 'practice'. In the beginning of your journey, you may need to cultivate the ability for endurance. The massage sequences flow seamlessly together, once you have mastered the methodology and the process. Whenever we learn something new, there is often awkwardness or 'clunkiness' to it. As you concentrate on 'getting it right', you may tense up and become exhausted. Whenever you notice your body tensing up, take a deep breath and exhale audibly. When you concentrate too intently, or when you do not exercise correct flow and position, it adds strain on your body. Take a deep breath and exhale completely.

Chapter 11:

Successful Intentional Ingredients

PRESENCE

THE CONSCIOUS PRESENCE OF both partners will make a vast difference. The masseur will need to communicate with their partner, listening to any sounds they make and watching their movements, reminding them to breathe. Encourage them to keep their eyes a little open. This will help them to be present and be able to heal in some cases. In case of an early trauma or an abuse, some people dissociate and become cut off from their bodies as a way of surviving the ordeal; for example, some people dissociate by 'checking out' when they are in a dentist's chair.

As the giver, you will need to be 'natural, loose, and empty', so that you can embody being a clear channel, like a hollow bamboo. Remember that even though the person you are massaging may not be fully present in their body, he/she is a god or a goddess, Shiva or Shakti, and it is your call to be present and witness this. During the massage, it is advisable to be engaged entirely with every ounce of your being, as if nothing else exists in the world but your partner.

Thich Nhat Hanh said in the book *Dharma in the Dishes*:

> If while washing dishes we think only of the cup of tea that awaits us, thus hurrying to get the dishes out of the way, we are not alive during the time we wash the dishes. We are completely

incapable of realizing the miracle of life. We will only be thinking of other things, barely aware. Thus we are sucked away into the future and are incapable of actually living one minute of life. Every act is a rite of mindfulness.

When you physically interact closely with another, you need to be aware that you are entering their personal space and that you must do so gently. You need to ask permission from their higher self to enter their aura, which is their energy body. You need to let go of any expectations of the outcome. You will be guided on your journey, exploring and facilitated by your sensitivity to their body's physical, emotional, and energetic responses. Whatever arises is perfect just as it is. It will help them in their journey. In tantra there is no 'good' or 'bad'; it just 'is'. So if an experience is disappointing, maybe they had expectations, or a story was being re-enacted that will never be fulfilled by reality. If we let go of expectations and remain in the present, then we can truly experience the ecstasy in every moment. Jean Pierre de Caussade wrote:

> If you abandon all restraint, carry your wishes to their furthest limits, open your heart boundlessly, there is not a single moment when you will not find everything you could possibly desire. The present moment holds infinite riches beyond your wildest dreams.

The mind is the seat of intelligence and wisdom, trust, and intuition. When cognitive thoughts interfere, your attention wanders from the massage, and this could be felt and perceived by the receiver as abandonment. Therefore you need to be confident and comfortable, even if you are not. You need to hold the intention and inwardly say something to the effect of, 'I am really intending to tune into you and focus 100 per cent on you. I regard you as a divine god/dess.'.

Since tantra is the weaving of energy and consciousness, we bring awareness through touch and touch through awareness. The intentions of the giver will be transferred energetically and through the touch.

People feel intentions. Hence it is important to be totally available to the receiver, acting like a clear vessel.

You are creating expansion, merging the energies and distributing the erotic charge all over the body. The feeling at the end of the massage can be one of extraordinary expansiveness, tingling all over and a sense as if the receiver has just 'touched the furthest edges of the universe', beyond the beyond, *Gate Gate*, as the universe has no boundaries that we know of. It is a profound space that may leave the receiver feeling as if they are basking in bliss, that they are 'no-thing'. It is important to watch the receiver during the massage; watch their face, as the receiver's expressions may change.

At the very end, it is vitally important to be present and attuned to the receiver. They may be basking in bliss but may need your gaze and presence to anchor them. Therefore at the end of the massage, sit quietly at their side, without touching them, and make sure you look at their face. Be totally attuned and attentive to them; they will feel you with them.

Resist looking around or getting on with chores. When they eventually open their eyes, your presence and compassionate gaze is most important and grounding. The receiver may experience emotional freedom and release, as they are being witnessed without judgments. They are being held in a safe contained space.

Testimonial

I have just had my fourth session, and each one has been a blissful and mind-opening experience, and each has been a completely different blend of physical sensuality and healing insight. I am constantly amazed at how you manage to find the words that cut to the core of my emotional needs that help unblock and heal them. After being worshiped by your eyes, your singing, and your being, I am able to really believe it. When I turned over after the back massage I was almost overwhelmed by the strong feelings of love I experienced as I looked up into your eyes. I am connecting with all the people in my life that I love and also with the whole universe. Thank you for the love that fills me up, thank you for the healing that cures my ills, and thank you for the bliss that revives and reinvigorates me. (S.H.)

HONOURING

The second very important ingredient to ensure the success of a tantric healing massage is the intention of honouring. Honour the receiver on all levels of their being. As you honour them, you are actually honouring yourself. As in all spiritual teachings there is no separation. What you do to others, you do to yourself. When we hurt someone, we hurt ourselves.

This sequence allows the giver to appreciate and honour the body of a real divine human being Shiva or Shakti. It honours all the five levels of being, corresponding to the five chakras in the Tibetan teachings.

1. **Physical.** The first level is the physical level of your being, which correlates to the first and second chakras in the Hindu tradition. Every part of your body is being massaged and integrated into one. All splitting, disjointing, or disconnection between your limbs and emotions are reconnected and aligned via the energy pathways of meridians and *nadis*. The flow of the massage will create integration, including all parts of the body. All parts are regarded as equal, all divine.

2. **Emotional.** The second level is the emotional level of your being. This correlates to the second and third chakras in the Hindu tradition. The physical well-being affects the emotions, and vice versa. Some people seek tantric healing massage therapy due to stress they may experience at work, in life, or in relationships. Others may experience emotional imbalance or physical conditions that may be acute and in

need of immediate attention. Some people may have chronic conditions that they may have been enduring for a while. These may be real or imagined, as some chronic conditions are induced in the mind, though the mind and emotions perceive this as real and it is experienced as such.

3. **Psychological.** The third level of your being is the psychological level. There is an overlap with the second intention of healing the body and mind, a desire to reach balance and harmony. This is mainly the fourth chakra, the heart chakra, as well as the second and third. It is concerned with unconditional love, equanimity, acceptance, compassion, and 'compersion'. Compersion is the word used to describe the celebration of another's success or erotic empathy and delight for the other, a selfless generosity of being.

4. **Intellectual.** The intellectual level is the fourth level of your being, residing in the fifth chakra at the throat and the sixth chakra at the third eye. It is concerned with speaking the truth and the resolution of karmic issues as well as understanding, awareness, wisdom and consciousness.

5. **Spiritual**. The fifth level of your being is the spiritual. It is connected to the seventh chakra at the crown, where you are connected to the whole of existence, where you are that which never changes. 'We are all spiritual beings having a human experience,' said Teilhard de Chardin.

Honouring yourself is the first step in being able to honour others. How can you give to others what you do not have for yourself? When you have compassion towards yourself, you will be able to give to others without being depleted. When you are embodying love, you will be able to give love unconditionally without resentments. On airplanes all over the world, the instructions are to put on the breathing mask to save yourself first, and then you can help others.

This is being 'intelligently selfish'. The Dalai Lama said:

> We can't be useful to ourselves unless we're useful to others. Whether we like it or not, we're all connected, and it is unthinkable to be happy all by oneself. Anyone concerned only by his own well-being will suffer eventually. Anyone concerned with the well-being of others takes care of himself without thinking about it. Even if we decide to remain selfish, let us be intelligently selfish – let us help others.

Case Study

> One of my clients, a down to earth mechanic, was encouraged to do homework of *namaste*-ing himself. *Namaste* is a gesture of honouring the divinity within, with the hands at a prayer position by the heart and the head slightly bowed. He reported that when he saw it demonstrated he did not realize the power of transformation and the profound effect it would have on his life. He was on anti-depressant medications for five years, and after doing this practice he feels the joy in life, his soul's purpose connection.

Testimonial

> If everyone could experience tantra there could be so much less pain in the world. Maybe one day when we are more developed. You have created a wonderfully safe space to explore … I have tears as I write this for the needless pain we cause to each other out of fear (R.)

INTENTION

Intention is the third most important ingredient in a genuine tantric massage. The receiver's intentions and goals should be honoured, and the giver's intention is one of honouring and worshipping, upholding, regarding the woman as the queen/goddess/empress and the man as the king/god/emperor.

Safety during the session is paramount. Agreements are to be adhered to, regardless of any desires that may arise in the moment. This will be determined initially, stating the boundaries that are required to be placed in order to create safety.

The giver will need to be clear about the receivers' intentions and will need to be in their heart, coming from a place of unconditional love. It is important to express verbally the intention, as the giver will remind the receiver of the intentions throughout the session.

HEALING

Healing can be a spontaneous side effect of a tantric healing massage. You can learn to cultivate high sexual arousal and the ability to master ejaculation control or ejaculatory choice. This will result in increased dopamine levels, which are the 'happy feel-good' neurotransmitters (which can help in cases such as Parkinson's disease).

Tantric healing massage can facilitate healing on all levels: physical, emotional, psychological, intellectual, and spiritual. The body may carry traumatic memory at a cellular level. Touch can heal and release energies that are deeply ingrained in the body. The intention of healing on the five levels of your being is actually a side effect, a by-product that happens spontaneously in a tantric healing massage, by bringing awareness and energy. A person's Ayurvedic constitution, the different qualities of *vatta, pitta, katha* or a combination of these, will also help determine what treatment is best.

Many men have an emotional release after or during the tantric healing massage. Some are moved to tears. For some men, this may be the first time they have been held and accepted and listened to, and that in itself could be overwhelming. Most men are relieved to be able to be real without inhibitions and to share intimate details they may have carried for many years. It is a real privilege and an honour to be able to facilitate this form of healing that literally frees them from the burdens of shame, guilt, and abuse. The massage is normally carried out in devotional chanting or silence, though if there is a need on the part of the receiver to communicate, that is very welcome. Ordinarily, the talking part is in the beginning to help gather information and express wishes and concerns. During the massage, the chants and silence helps the receiver enter into an altered state of consciousness.

Testimonial

> My mind is still catching up, but it feels like something quite deep happened. Thanks for being there, amplifying Presence and helping me to give myself permission to consciously separate myself more from an unholy umbilical cord with the past. This is real deep stuff, and it has affected me quite a bit. So it has been quite an intense time. At the same time, though, I also have wonderful glimpses of how it feels to be free from the grip of this (mother's) claw. The abdomen massage seems to be quite powerful. (E.V.)

Tantric transmutation of energy and learning to retain semen will do wonders. It reverses the ageing process, as well as allowing sexual performance to last much longer. You can direct and spread erotic energy to facilitate healing intentionally. You can arouse and direct the sexual energy, which has the potency of healing and rejuvenation, consciously sending the energy to the areas that require the healing.

Sometimes a touch may be experienced by the receiver as if the area touched is numb or feels as if it is deadened. Should this occur, the masseur can help re-energize the area by going back to an area nearby where there is sensitivity. You then stroke or tap from that area towards the desensitized area, gradually connecting and enlivening it, bringing the sensitivity in to awaken the numbness. This could be occurring due to some form of previous abuse.

Surgery could have left somatic memories in the body, experienced abusive, on physical and emotional levels. At times doctors treat parts of the body or the whole being as a thing rather than a complete human being. This can have a huge effect on the healing process and could scar the person. It has been observed in an experiment at one hospital, where doctors acknowledged the patients with a greeting and listened to them, that the recovery was much faster.

Case Study 1

An enterprising young man in his early thirties came to see me as a last act of desperation. He had been involved in a car crash and was lucky to be alive. He had suffered from serious pain in his back and shoulder, and the doctor wanted to give him steroids and a cocktail of drugs to manage the pain. We set the intention for the healing and the area to direct the kundalini energy. He was barely able to lay on the treatment surface. He had a strap around his shoulder and was clearly in pain. I helped guide him in the process and within less than half an hour, his body relaxed, the pain dissolved, and he was able to move his arm freely. Every three weeks he returned to top up the treatment, which was more pleasant than his hospital physiotherapy and more effective.

Testimonial (by the above client)

My experiences of your tantric massages have been incredible. On my first experience I was slightly nervous, which I feel inhibited my energy. I was immediately convinced of the power of my energy which you have channelled.

> My second experience was bliss. I experienced the power of my sexual energies for the first time ever. It woke up my sexual energy, and I had completed 1.5 hours of multi-orgasmic rushes. My breathing was deep and allowed my energy to flow to every part of my body. I experienced the gateway for the first time. It felt wonderful and I felt powerful. It re-energized my whole body.
>
> In my third experience it was something close to an out-of-body experience. With a key focus on healing my damaged ribs, you channelled the sexual energy to these areas specifically, and it was an incredible result. I hobbled into the session with pain at

(due to the accident) 7-8 and walked out on zero – completely without any pain at all. I connected very deeply, and the energies sparked powerful waves of orgasmic properties. My delight was the depth and the power of the energies. I experienced an out-of-body experience that felt more powerful than anything I've ever felt.

I can feel the energies flowing through my body, my body come alive. I'm experiencing the power of my sexual energies and channelling this to my ribs and back, and the body is healing. I can control the climax to create multiple waves of orgasmic energy. (B.F.)

Case Study 2

A female client came to see me as a last resort, suffering from chronic back pain which escalated and forced her to take three weeks off from her job at one of the top advertising companies in the UK. Frightened of experiencing more pain, every time she went to a chiropractor in an attempt to alleviate the symptoms, she felt worse. She melted and the pain dissipated naturally when I touched her back in a way she has never experienced before. She was amazed at the ease of the resolution.

Testimonial

Thank you for your love and caring … I felt very held and seen with all my rubbish/vulnerability/fear, etc., and yet still treated as an adult who on some level knew how to take care of herself and her needs. I do appreciate your support. The experience is so … ethereal. Suffice to say … **yes** and **yes** to doing more' (D., a female therapist)

Post-Partum Sexuality

After childbirth, post-partum sexuality can be helped through caring conscious touch. Trauma can be held in the body following medical intervention, such as gynaecological operations and procedures which may have caused shock to the mother.

The scar tissue holds the memories and may be too sensitive; even the womb may hold vulnerability, affecting sexuality, and may interfere with the possibility of enjoying sexual intimacy and orgasms. Where doctors have not treated patients with warmth or considered a patient's worries, they may have felt traumatized emotionally. They may have felt that the only way to cope with and endure the medical intervention is by dissociation.

Stress

Tantric healing massage helps people who are dealing with enormous volumes of stress. The methods shared here have helped thousands of people regain confidence in their sexuality and the hope and courage to really engage in life. This work is most humbling, and it is an honour to help and be the catalyst of change.

Case Study

I was able to help transform the lives of several sex workers. One lady was working as an escort. After our session she became a life coach, empowering people in large institutes. Her life turned round 180 degrees. Some women seek resolution, acceptance, and forgiveness to help them come to terms with the path they have chosen, and they seek a way to heal their past wounds and transform their lives.

Testimonial

I arrived home now, feeling like you have held my hand and guided me though the questions I had and that you have helped me look at them with the clarity and honesty I desired. My mind is at peace and my heart is resting! Thank you for being there and listening. I am so glad I saw you today. (T.K.)

DEALING WITH ISSUES AND CONDITIONS

It takes a lot of courage to take action towards the resolution. Making the first call or starting an email dialogue may be the hardest thing you need to do. The initial fear of reaching out to seek help is worse than the reality of dealing with the issues. It takes more energy to try to keep the issues from rising to the surface than to resolve them.

People teaching, studying, and practicing tantric massage are to encourage the receiver to communicate any such conditions as much as possible, prior to the massage commencing and during the massage if the receiver feels the need. When starting a massage, all conditions, afflictions, medical history, and current states of being and feelings need to be communicated and addressed before any touch commences. All personal boundaries need to be communicated honestly, as well as any expectations, hopes, and wishes.

The strength of tantric healing massage may lie in its ability to bring about healing naturally, even if the receiver is not consciously aware of any issues or stories during the session. Sacred sexual healing practiced with integrity and intention has the potent power of creation and resolution.

LOVE PARTNERSHIPS

For healing the relationship in a love partnership, it is highly advisable to embark upon this journey together, as doing so can help create deeper intimacy and honesty and strengthens the bond. The tantric path is called the thunder-bolt lightening path, Vajrayana Buddhism, and it is regarded as the fastest path of enlightenment, because it embraces all aspects of our being, including our sexuality and relationships. Therefore this tantric path should come with a health warning: this will change your life! It will be advisable to embark upon it with your beloved, as it will take you to higher planes that you never envisaged, and to depths of your being you never knew existed.

Should you choose to follow the tantric path on your own while you are in an intimate committed relationship, please be aware that you will be catapulted to a faster spiritual evolution path. If you embark upon this journey without your love partner, your trajectory will vary greatly from your partner's, who may be travelling through life in a familiar, predicable, and slower orbit. This will be amplified and will be evident in the relationship.

Through tantric practices you can harmonize your relationship and propel it to a whole new dimension. As mentioned before, it can even reawaken and rekindle the spark of love and sexuality in long-term relationships that may have fallen into the familiarity and taking-for-granted trap. This requires commitment and dedication to yourself, the beloved, and the practices.

ETHICAL CONDUCT

Ethical conduct is vitality important, especially when working with women clients. We must ensure that they are aware of the emotional repercussions. Here is a statement and agreement Martin Jelfs and I use:

> Tantric healing massage releases powerful energies and is a fast therapeutic process that is facilitated through masculine presence and touch. It uses a warm, accepting, honouring, and totally non-judgmental witnessing of your process, whilst holding the space and creating safety. Along with this, we use a type of touch which touches you deeply energetically and physically, awakening and allowing energy to begin to move.

Energies locked deeply in your body and psyche can be simply pleasurable and even blissful; both are profoundly healing. It is also possible that past traumas are touched – including a sense of what you have missed. These may have been repressed and forgotten and are emerging to be healed because, at last, the right conditions are here; safety, an unshakable presence and skill. At last a giver arrives who can honour and receive all your feelings so you can really let go. This allows you to move through to your desire, bliss, joy and passion for life.

Rumi Poetry

Passion makes the old medicine new.

Passion lops off the bough of weariness.

Passion is the elixir that renews:

How can there be weariness

When passion is present?

Oh, don't sigh heavily from fatigue.

Seek passion, seek passion, and seek passion!

(Mathnawi VI, 4302-4304 www.romanticlovesecrets.com/
Passion-Makes-Old-Medicine-New-Poems.html)

THE IMPORTANCE OF CONTINUITY

All this can happen in one session, but often an intense experience can be followed by emotions such as feelings of shame and various forms of self-attack, which can easily lead back into repression and hiding. For this reason it is best to have a series of sessions so that you have a solid sense of being accompanied on your journey. A good practitioner will contact you a day after a session to share the emotions and feelings awakened by the previous day's session.

It is important that you have a sense of a continuing presence and a solid relationship to hold you – particularly if you do not have this anywhere else in your life. The relationship can enable you to work through what is coming up, as early trauma is usually very connected to relationship and also to joy and bliss. It is best witnessed and shared as an anchoring reparative experience. Healing is a process, a journey which you were not able to do alone.

The regularity of the sessions provides a container to go deeper to the roots of the blocks or traumas. This does not necessarily involve painful emotions; often after touching a trauma or traumatic pattern, they can be healed through pleasure when consciousness is really present.

After an initial session to meet and gather information and have a taste of the process, a good practitioner will need to have a commitment to a series of sessions to create the container to allow the alchemy of tantric bodywork to succeed. A total of seven sessions usually allows for this process and can also give some focus on different issues at the seven different chakras. A good frequency for the work is fortnightly with at least a phone call or email exchange in between. This is a very powerful process over three months

Testimonials

Thank you for your patience, support, and understanding. We have never been through such strong rivers. We have felt great shifts in our relationship. The biggest part of that shift happened with me – smiling – thank you for taking your time with me after a weekend of giving. It has changed my very basic experience, my 'evolution', and in doing so, my relationship with my partner. There are no words to thank you. (A.S.)

The more I come to see you, the more I open up, the more I feel that I respond, the more I am willing to explore and experience still further. (I.J.)

AGREEMENTS

There is a basic agreement we use with clients. It could be along the following lines.

'As we are working with tantric healing bodywork and massage, which at present is outside conventional therapy, we want to ensure that you understand the nature of this powerful approach.

'Our simple intention from this work is to speed your healing, growth, and empowerment at all levels of your being. This work involves us directly touching and massaging your body from a place of honouring, respect, and awareness. This touch may include your genitals, and we will seek your permission before doing this and before touching you internally. We are working with physical, emotional, sexual, and spiritual energies.

'We need you to breathe, feel, express, be present, and be authentic. We will remind you about this and call you back to yourself if you forget. We need you not to have taken non-prescription drugs or alcohol for at least twelve hours before the session.

'We need to know if you have a history of physical or sexual abuse that you are aware of, a recent history of psychiatric treatments, or if you are currently taking any kind of medications or have any infections (including herpes which may currently be inactive) or any health issues.

'None of this need prevent our work together, but knowing about it may help us to work out what is best for you. Massage may not be appropriate for some health conditions. We can use gloves if it is necessary or if you would like. We generally use organic raw coconut oil and sweet almond oil.

'We will keep our work together absolutely confidential within the limits of the law, only using anonymous information for professional supervision purposes. See the ethics statement which gives some more information on transcendence websites: www.tantra.uk.com or www.tantric-healing-massage.com and www.shivoham.asia.'

DIALOGUE

During the massage the receiver will need to communicate what is happening if something is surfacing emotionally or if memories are triggered. This will help release them naturally and safely.

Encourage the receiver to look at you so that they can see that they are being witnessed, unless this takes them out of their process. This is a most powerful healing process. For someone to enjoy a sensual tantric massage and be witnessed at their heightened sexual arousal or emotional release can be experienced as profoundly healing.

Make sure you know of any sensitivities or allergies beforehand, including contra-indications to massage such as some cancers, blood clots, thrombosis, etc.

Testimonial

I think my mind is still trying to catch up with what happened this afternoon. Like being in some kind of a daze mentally. My body feels refreshed, nourished, and serenely calm, and I can feel my whole body as one field of pulsing – or purring – energy, complete unto itself. What was so important for me was the inclusion of the genitals as part of a whole body experience. To lovingly and caringly validate and integrate this area into a whole body experience is a most healing gift for a man. (E.V.)

CHAPTER 12:

Aspects of Healing

BE AWARE OF THE following common aspects in healing, applicable to both the giver and the receiver.

DISSOCIATION

SOME SEXUAL HEALERS AND sex workers have a tendency to override their own emotional needs and well-being. This is by no mean a judgment on their life choices but rather an observation from listening to many sexual healers who have come to see me for help and therapy.

Sometimes people cut off from their own bodies and emotions as a survival mechanism, to help them carry out intimate acts with people they are not connected with emotionally or attracted to, perhaps even repulsed by. The reasons for this kind of behaviour are complex, whether they may be forced by other people or by their own choice.

The reality of dissociation, denial, and projection is common in many people. Cutting off from the body may help in the short term to endure an ordeal, just as most of us do in dental or medical procedures. It is also used to survive physical and emotional abuse such as rape or war crimes.

In the long term, overcoming dissociation will require the commitment to heal and the willingness to look at and release the trauma via psychosexual, psychotherapy, and body therapy de-armouring. Be mindful to seek professional help from qualified or well-established practitioners.

Remember to honour your temple of mind-body-soul and honour your boundaries. Listen to your soul's needs: your soul talks to you via your body and your emotions. You know when you are on the right path of your soul's purpose, as you are connected to the joy of the soul. When you are not, you are wallowing in misery. You may connect to your soul's purposes by enjoying solving challenges or helping people. Your purposes are unique and there are more than one.

PARKINSON'S DISEASE

When working with clients who have Parkinson's condition, cultivating the practice of ejaculation control and ejaculatory choice actually brings about a relief from the constant shaking when medications are not taken. Of course, if you are taking medications, please continue to do so and consult your doctor or a specialist.

The practice of high sexual arousal without ejaculation means that the dopamine levels the brain produces into the body are increased. These are the happy feel-good hormones, the natural chemical excreted by the brain, and they help to quieten and calm the body as the shaking subsides. I have witnessed amazing results with some clients of total temporary reversal of the condition by simply being present with them and allowing them to experience sexual energy as a healing medium. To ensure this is permanent will depend on the client committing and practicing what they have been taught.

Case Study

An interesting incident happened with a client, as his doctor recommended he might benefit from a series of tantric healing sessions. He'd had Parkinson's disease for six years following the death of his brother, which he felt was his responsibility. He was taking medication to help with the worst of the symptoms.

While he was receiving a back massage he was able to relax sufficiently as I was stroking from the head down, crossing my hands so my left hand was stroking his right side, and my right hand was touching the left side of his head. I noticed the shaking had stopped completely.

When I changed to stroking on the back, the shaking started gently but on the other side. He seemed to have switched sides. The shaking stopped completely when I employed movements that encourage balancing and harmonizing polarities and also when he was unable to follow my movements with his mind. When he was able to follow my hands with his mind and be in control, the shaking re-erupted. I was monitoring this and was able to predict with accuracy when the switch would happen, observing the power of his brain at work.

Testimonial

It is an experience that I will not forget in a long time. I really felt so safe in your hands and at the end I felt as if I had known you for a long time instead of just a couple of hours. Your smiling face during the session was really infectious. It was a really tender and loving experience and something I have never experienced before. I went home feeling rejuvenated and ready to 'take on the world'. I know that your treatment will indirectly help my dear but disabled wife in that I feel renewed and better able to help her with her problems. (N.D.)

TETANY

Some who may have had fear or trauma, tend to experience tetany as a reaction during the massage; it is be a body response to an emotional trauma.

Tetany is an involuntary contraction of the muscles. It occurs normally as a response to fear or tension, as well as not breathing correctly and exhaling excessively.

MENOPAUSE AND ANDROPAUSE

There is a lot of misunderstanding about the menopause, mistakenly thought of as a female condition only which is dishonouring of male. Andropause is the male menopause, also known as the low-T. The decline in testosterone levels contributes to this phenomena. Andropause symptoms consist of fatigue, sexual dysfunctions, weight gain, mood changes, or depression.

However, this is an urban myth which we play along with. This period could be experienced as a blessing. Menopausal women can enjoy much more liberated sexual expression and are not concerned with the menstrual cycle. Receiving tantric healing massage during the menopause could be another way to manage their emotional wellbeing in a holistic way. Of course, if you are taking medication, please consult your doctor. Rapid temperature change (hot flushes) is one of the symptom's indicators.

VAGINISMUS

This is a condition some women have as a body response to attempted penetration, resulting in pain experienced due to physical or emotional trauma. It results in a vaginal contraction, causing distress, discomfort, pain and prevents penetration. This extreme reaction can be due to a history of emotional or physical abuse, as well as associations with events. It would be advisable to seek professional help from a psychosexual therapist or a professional reputable tantric masseur, as there are several effective ways to overcome this issue.

This can also traumatize the man, as he may feel rejected by not understanding the cause of the symptoms.

CANCER, AGING, AND ALTERNATIVE THERAPIES

Please seek traditional professional medical advice. The books *Prostate Health in 90 Days Without Drugs* and *Surgery: Cure Your Prostate Now Without Drugs or Surgery* by Larry Clapp are highly recommended for all people to realize that they do have control and they can do something about their lives and prostate cancer.

Case Studies

Three women clients who came to see me all had terminal cancers and were given limited time to live. One flew more than 3,000 miles to see me. They say the reason they lived years after the doctor's predicted dates was their determination to succeed, taking charge of their own lives by altering their diet, supplementing with nutrients and vitamins, and receiving complimentary therapies. They resolved not to accept the verdict, and now they live to tell their story and enjoy their lives travelling around the world.

It is often the case that people experience cancer as a social and personal stigma. People are afraid to touch those who have cancer either because of an irrational fear, as if it is a contagious condition or because of the fear of being sued. Touch is so important to our well-being; without it we wither and die.

Ageing clients seek tantric healing massage, as it may be the only form of touch they get. They are starved of our basic human need. Often people who are dying are desperate to be touched. Since life is a terminal condition, why deprive them of the most important part of their being, where they feel the caring touch over the whole of the body? They feel honoured, nourished, and loved since the hands giving are an extension of the heart.

The power of belief can be profound and life-changing. The belief in the Madonna can transform people and heal their dis-ease. Many books have been written about this subject, and you need to find what you believe in or choose a new set of beliefs that will help you on this journey.

The mind is phenomenally powerful. Astronauts prepare with the mind to go into space. Athletes harness the power of the mind to win races and competitions. Some individuals have surgery using hypnosis in place of anaesthetic.

Please ensure you seek professional advice from traditional allopathic medical professionals and complementary therapists. There are many stories of individuals who overcame severe conditions and illnesses. There are documented stories in films that are easily accessible through the media. You are the greatest expert on yourself, so trust your intuition as to which alternative therapy can best complement the traditional approach.

Recently a large supermarket chain published a free booklet on testicular cancer, which had nothing to do with products they sell – excellent marketing and socially responsible.

Testimonial

Such a caring and liberating massage. I feel very positive about the future (prostate cancer operation) with your support. (F.D.B.)

FIBROIDS

These are mostly common benign tumours inside the uterus. Leiomyoma is a uterine fibroid. The symptoms may be pain during the moon cycle, menstruation, pain during sexual intimacy, or frequent urge to urinate. It is rare for fibroids to impede during pregnancy. Some people prefer to cut them out of the body, but some women have made peace with them and find the source of their ability to heal themselves. Always take proper advice from qualified medical practitioners and ask for second opinions.

OEDEMA

Oedema is an abnormal swelling in the body under the skin and in cavities, where the balance of fluids will need to be readdressed by the removal of secretion of fluids. It is known as dropsy or hydropsy.

CYSTITIS

Cystitis is a urinary bladder infection in the bladder which has infected the urethra. The most common cause is a bacterial infection which is easily treatable.

ERECTILE DYSFUNCTION

Erectile dysfunction could be a result of many contributory factors. Nowadays there are more soya products in food, and the dosage may act as the equivalent of birth-control pills. The water in some parts of the world is also contributing to the reduction in male hormones. The medications that are prescribed in some cases as a precautionary measure for controlling blood pressure, cholesterol levels, or diabetes also have an effect on erections.

In this era of the internet, we are blessed with a lot of free knowledge available at our finger tips. It has also accentuated porn exploitation, resulting in sexual dysfunctions and miseducation. Most erectile dysfunctions are due to porn desensitization of our arousal states. Some people now can only achieve erection or climax when watching pornography on the internet.

CHAPTER 13:

The Big O

THE ORGASMIC PLATEAU – EROTIC TRANCE

YOU CAN LEARN HOW to cultivate the experience of the orgasmic plateau – also known as an erotic trance – and how to harness the energies of high sexual charge and transmute and amplify orgasms. The practices shared in this book and also in the second and third book in this series and the DVDs will enable both men and women to experience multiple orgasms.

Learning to master this phenomenon is also known as 'riding the wave of bliss'. It occurs at the point of pre-ejaculation. With practice, you can learn to extend the time you spend on the orgasmic plateau.

As with all practices, you would, for example, in order to improve your performance and muscle tone, dedicate time to work out regularly in the gymnasium. The same applies to your love muscles, and you can learn more about this later on in the book.

The orgasmic plateau can occur by raising energy and enabling you to experience a whole-body orgasm by opening energy channels in the body and by activating the chakras. At the orgasmic plateau all senses are heightened. Time dilation is often experienced, where time feels as if it has stood still and at the same time has passed so fast. Five minutes can seem like five hours, and five hours appear to be as five minutes.

When this experience happens, you know you have been in a tantric time zone.

As the sexual charge is built up, the receiver may be vibrating on an orgasmic plateau, experiencing a state of being as if they are supercharged with profound energy that will have benefits beyond the imagination. Sexual release of these potent energies will result in an instant gratification, with the usual ejaculation for a man. This is the usual case in which the climax itself, paradoxically, will be turned into an anti-climax. This is often followed by a feeling of unfulfilment and disappointment and could also lead to feeling disinterested in the partner and result in a lack of energy and sleepiness. *Post coitus triste* is a condition frequently described in art and literature.

Grasping at a quick release will dissipate the supercharged energies that help us move away from genital-concentrated genital-centric orgasms into whole-body orgasms. This metaphor illustrates the point: A man is on his way to the Ritz, where a delicious 'festival to the taste buds' banquet is being held in his honour. He is very hungry and desires to gratify his addiction (his hunger) instantly (like an ejaculation). A short distance from the hotel he stops at a fast-food stall and gorges himself. He will still be able to enjoy some of the feast, but now the subtle flavours will be totally wasted on him.

The subtle but profound multiple orgasms that are available to all men if they are willing to experience and learn to amplify them, will be beyond description if you let go of the addiction to fast ejaculation. These multiple orgasms will become stronger as you practice and master tantric healing massages and ejaculation control. A man could allow himself to experience orgasms that are not based on physical contraction but on relaxing and expanding more, yielding to the orgasms that are based deeper in the body in the male sacred G spot, or in the heart centre and other places in the body. This will enable men to experience a deep state of profound bliss and full satiation that can last for days on end.

To Ejaculate or Not to Ejaculate? That Is the Question!

What is an orgasm? The dictionary definition is, 'the physical and emotional sensation experienced at the peak of sexual excitation, usually resulting from stimulation of the sexual organ and usually accompanied in the male by ejaculation' (http://dictionary.reference.com/browse/orgasm). It is far more than just a relief like a sneeze. It is a full-body experience that can be experienced in the whole being. It is a most phenomenal experience that is at times beyond description. Words belittle the magnitude of what you experience. A full-body orgasm can feel as if it sends you to all corners of the universe, where you experience oneness with all that is.

It is a common mistake to think that male ejaculations are orgasms. Orgasm and ejaculation are not the same. They are two separate physiological occurrences within the body. They are very different from each other both in a felt experience and in their neurology.

Orgasm, in French *le petit mort*, means 'the little death'. It is a preparation for the ultimate death, the ultimate orgasm when we unite with all that is and enter into a new realm. It can also be the death of the ego, which helps spiritual development. However, the ego will be resurrected as you drop out of the bliss state. What occurs at the moment of orgasm is that the brain is producing and excreting dopamine at a high input level, which feels wonderful, as if you are invincible. Dopamine has double-edged sword characteristics. Since it is a pleasure-seeking hormone, it may take you over the edge, resulting in ejaculation.

When ejaculation occurs, the same areas in the brain light up as when heroin is taken. (See articles at www.reuniting.info.) Orgasm occurs prior to ejaculation, at the point of the peak of excitement. Male ejaculation could at times be experienced as an anti-climax and be disappointing to the man. Ejaculation ordinarily means 'game over', where you will be missing out on the exquisite flavours of multiple orgasms. Ejaculation normally follows immediately after an orgasm, though male ejaculation could occur without a man reaching orgasm. It is also true that a man can experience orgasms without ejaculation, even without having an erection. Many men experience dry orgasms before puberty.

Our society puts a lot of emphasis on performance in the bedroom. The competition that is encouraged at school and in the media affects young men, and they are concerned about both their performance and, literally, how they measure up. Pressure to perform is the affliction of our era and can destroy confidence. This can have repercussions that permeate every aspect of your being and can affect your work life and relationships. For some individuals it is the cause of chronic ailments.

Enjoy basking in the orgasmic plateau. This will take practice, and you may be pleasantly surprised at the amount of energy and vitality you will gain. You will also be like a walking magnet, being attractive to people and also circumstances. This is a 'magic' power generator over which you have total control and can use once you have experimented and learnt the skill of ejaculatory choice.

The male G-spot prostate massage can help prevent prostate cancer and can facilitate male multiple orgasms (MMO). MMO could be experienced when a man refrains from the ordinary ejaculation-based thrill. Instead of releasing and diffusing the erotic charge by losing his seed, he can transmute and sublimate the energies, experiencing MMO or 'injaculation', which will be explained in further detail in the next section.

Each time you have an orgasm or are riding the wave of bliss, it is penetrating another chakra and going through. Sometimes you can get the sense that you are piercing through something, sometimes as if you are dissolving into everything. In addition to directing the energy up the chakras, you can also redirect the orgasmic energy to a particular area or organ to which you wish to send potent healing sexual energy.

If you consider the orgasm as the peak experience at number 8, where sleep state is 0 and 10 describes the state of being completely spent and fully ejaculated, 9 would be the ejaculation. Imagine a peak like an upwards triangle or a summit with the figure 8 at the top. That is the orgasm. When ejaculation starts, it is a point of no return. The downhill drop follows, and it can be experienced as an anti-climax.

By relaxing at the point of 8, the orgasm peak, you can create an orgasmic plateau experience instead of a peak orgasm. Both you and your partner will learn to 'stalk' the energy and harness it. You can visualize this as a 'table' mountain. Relax at 8 and together with the practitioner or your love partner direct the sexual energy in your body and spread the energy so it is not just concentrated in the genitals. You can then experience basking in the orgasmic plateau, where you may stay for what can seem like an eternity riding the waves of bliss. The waves will just keep lapping at the shore of your being. The more you relax and let go, the more you can experience this erotic charge.

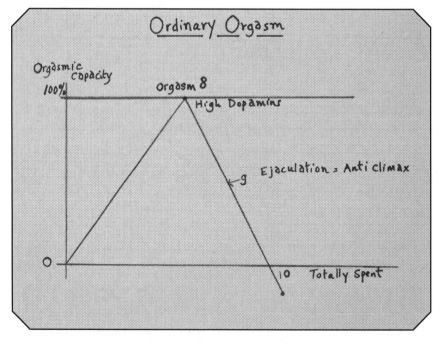

Image 24: Orgasms Graph

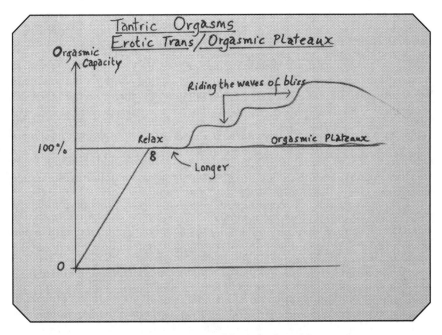

Image 25: Orgasmic Table Mountain Plateaux

In ordinary ways of love-making or masturbation, men experience tension building up in the body. They will tense the body until the only way out for the energy to relieve the tension is to ejaculate. In tantra we encourage the man to relax more. The more you relax, the more you can contain. The more you relax and let go, the more space you create for the new to come in, and the more sexual energy you can experience. This will become evident as you practice relaxation in the midst of sexual arousal; thus your orgasmic capacity increases.

By exercising relaxation in the most heightened sexual arousal, what used to be your 100 per cent orgasmic capacity will now become your 50 or 70 per cent orgasmic level. You could actually experience this and the higher states of arousal and bliss if you practice. The orgasms will become more profound, stronger, and longer-lasting. This is true for both men and women. This experience will only be tantric if the orgasmic bliss is intertwined with awareness.

Awareness is the platform upon which the orgasm will occur, like waves on a shore. Without the three actions of clear awareness, sublimation, and dedication, it will not be tantric but rather hedonistic. Without these three actions or intentions, the desire for bigger and multiple orgasms will be the grasping of the ego and fuel addictive behaviour.

Overcoming the addiction to male ejaculation can liberate you to experience the states of erotic trance, or the orgasmic plateau, for hours at a time. This is superior to and beyond any orgasms based in ejaculation. Both men and women need to overcome this male ejaculation misconception through educating and reacquainting themselves with sexuality.

Society still frowns upon sexual exploration. Even though we may think of ourselves as sexually liberated, there are still judgmental attitudes encountered everywhere. The use of sexuality as portrayed in the media also contributes to this misguidance. Some of it is founded in the misuse and abuse of power by individuals, while some of it is due to lack of sexual and emotional maturity.

The porn industry is one of the most profitable industries even in times of recession. There are few people in the porn industry who enjoy what they do, and the majority have to cut off from their feelings to survive it, either by emotional dissociation or by the aid of narcotic drugs. As the body is the temple of the soul, when we cut off from the body, we deny our soul its birth right, the joy of being.

Men have had a lifetime of practicing quick ejaculation due to early sexual practices where they had to learn by trial and error to have quick release before they might be caught by a parent, sibling, or peer and be humiliated or punished for exploring something that is so natural and necessary. This is due to cultural and religious dogmas.

It has been proven scientifically that the regions of the brain that deal with addictive narcotics are associated with the experience of ejaculation. When a man ejaculates, the areas of the brain that light up are the same areas of the brain that light up when a person takes heroin. Being aware of this will enable the man to overcome the addiction to ejaculation and be able to begin to enjoy more fulfilling orgasms, and sustain deeper orgasmic states that will result in more durable love-making skills and happier intimate relationships.

Women also have their part in inducing ejaculation in men. This could be due to their own need for fulfilment. Some women over-stimulate men so they extract their semen as an unconscious act of power over them. The other reason some women want the men to ejaculate, other than the sexual thrill or the feeling of power over the men, is that on some intuitive level the woman senses that the ejaculate is potent with life force energy, the *ojas*. It has been proven scientifically that the ejaculate acts as an anti-depressant if absorbed, due to a chemical reaction inside her yoni or vulva.

A woman is responsible for her desires and boundaries, her own orgasm and appropriate conduct. If the woman is giving a tantric massage to a client, she needs to be sensitive and mindful of the contract and boundaries set out in the beginning. A woman has a lot of power when she is giving a tantric massage. Be mindful that it could be experienced as abusive if the woman forces the man to have an ejaculation. She needs to be attuned to his breathing and bodily responses. The patterns of reactions and facial expressions will help to gauge the intensity and rhythm. They will also determine when to direct the energy, and in which direction, to enable the man to experience erotic trance.

You can direct the energy towards the crown at the top of the head or to the third eye between the eyebrows. You can also ground the energy, stroking it towards the feet. Then spread the energy, as if you are anointing the whole of the body with this sublime force.

Sublimation is a tantric practice where you transform raw sexual energy into a refined expression of consciousness. What is an orgasm? A full body, whole-being orgasm that sends you to all corners of the universe, where you can experience oneness with all that is.

Testimonial

I realized that I had found what I had been looking for: the cradle of erotica. The split between my body and my soul was healed, and you were able to hold the powerful energy that was generated from this re-connection. A big part of why it worked was because it felt safe to take risks (paradox) and be open. (K.B.)

EXTENDED MASSIVE ORGASM: BECOMING MULTI-ORGASMIC MEN AND WOMEN

The intention is to enable men to experience becoming multi-orgasmic. It is a fact that all men have the capacity to become multi-orgasmic and to cultivate injaculation. Explore letting go of chasing ejaculation for instant gratification. This will facilitate experiencing multiple orgasms. They will be subtle to begin with. The more you practice ejaculatory choice and strengthening the pelvic-floor muscles, the stronger the orgasms will become. Stimulating the gateway to heaven will open up a whole new world of multiple orgasms and extended massive orgasm for men.

Women can also experience extended massive orgasm. This is more common, as women are able to have the valley orgasm, which lasts much longer and feels more wholesome and deeper. This is so profound that the rippling effect is felt all over the body, in the hands, the belly, the head, and the feet. Tantric healing massage pays close attention to all the limbs in a certain order. The sequence is preparing the body to contain these powerful energies to surge through. This could be experienced as an altered state of consciousness, a spiritual experience, healing, and emotional release. Stimulating the 'gateway to heaven' (the anus) will also open up a whole new world of multiple orgasms and extended massive orgasms for men.

Testimonials

'The effect after the session lasted for quite a few days. My sexual energy remains at the higher gear still now! (A.S.)

You have the ability to open doors I didn't even know were there! A very special experience' (F.D.B.)

INJACULATION

Injaculation is the process that can occur during the male orgasm, a re-absorption of the ejaculate into the body, resulting in heightened states of consciousness, healing, magnetism, and rejuvenation. Injaculation can be felt on a physical level as a most profound experience, far superior to ordinary genital-based ejaculation.

Testimonial

A truly liberating experience! Sensations were passing through me like a starburst. A very special moment. (F.D.B.)

For some men, the experience is just as if he has ejaculated, though without the loss of semen or energy. At times a man can feel as if he is experiencing an internal ejaculation like implosions inside the body. The body will then reabsorb the ejaculate as he uses the *moola bhanda*, the root lock (see the section on Your Love Muscles in chapter 15), as well as breathing and directing the energy upwards. This will create a vacuum which will draw the *ojas* back into the blood stream. *Ojas* is our life force energy in liquid form that is present in the sexual juices. For other men, injaculation could be felt deep in the body like implosions – internal explosions that are like human 'supernova' reenergizing your whole being.

Testimonial

I have done your self-pleasuring exercise a few times now and have really enjoyed it. I was able to injaculate, which seems to have given me a lot of energy. I still feel quite different, much freer inside, more inner space and assured, in touch with my own will power, feeling energy across the whole body energy. (E.V.)

Re-absorbing the *ojas* will result in creating healing, rejuvenation, and empowerment. You will become like a magnet and an antenna at the same time, attracting to you the things you desire, including situations and people that will enhance your life. The person experiencing the injaculation can carry on vibrating as the energy is rippling deliciously inside. These profound heightened experiences can sometimes continue for days afterwards. Some people experience this as *samadhi*. They may have the ability to connect to and awaken this state naturally in meditation.

The Chinese Taoists tantric practitioners achieve the experience of multiple orgasms rippling through the body by contracting at the moment of orgasm, tensing all muscles from head to toes, including face and internal muscles. Joseph Kramer, PhD, the great tantric sexuality educator in the United States and the founder of Body Electric, teaches the 'big draw' technique. While tensing the whole body, take a deep and full breath and hold it until you can hold it no longer and then, by relaxing, your body will be elevated into the orgasmic trance. You can also try this the other way round, where you take the big draw after you exhale, tensing all the muscles until you need to inhale and then let go.

Tantra is a science, where you are the scientist and the experiment at the same time. Even though the big draw is not specifically a tantric practice, it is certainly beneficial to experiment with. By adding the element of ritual and bringing awareness, you can transform it into a tantric practice.

Tantra is the path that puts an emphasis on surrender and relaxation. For some people, tensing paradoxically enables a deeper relaxation. Experiment and discover what works for you. Tantra advocates surrender in a blissful orgasmic way beyond time and space. *Gate Gate*, beyond the beyond.

Testimonial

I have now used your suggested *swastika mudra* meditation for a week or so, and would just like to report on the results. It seems to have increased the intensity of my 'no-thought state'. It feels like being aroused while meditating! Just like wanting to make love with the empty space! It's never happened with any other meditation, but it happens with this one! What a shift in my consciousness! (J.D.)

CHAPTER 14:

Dedication

MANIFESTING YOUR VISION USING SEX MAGIC

IT IS IMPORTANT TO dedicate a session to a desired outcome or as a spiritual dedication for the benefit of humanity. The profound energies that are released in the process are far too great to disperse without being utilized in a way that will be beneficial for yourselves and the world. The power that is being unleashed is beyond our ordinary understanding.

You can dedicate the session to a particular resolution of an affliction or to a particular outcome you desire to achieve. The image of what it is that you desire to achieve, short term or long term, or the image of your life accomplished is used as the focus of the meditation. Visualization is used to help manifestation and to focus the mind.

Establish your intentions and the needs of the receiver. Make sure you ask prior to commencing, as often people tend to assume they know, especially when it is their love partner. Even if you may have been together for a long time, make sure you ask. It will show that you care and are considerate, sensitive to their needs. People's aspirations and desires will change, either as they watch the desires as a meditation, or as they receive (or not) the object of desire. Over time priorities change. In long-term relationships people change, and so will their wishes.

The vision of the receiver is a vital ingredient. You will need to establish a vision for the receiver. Find out what it is they desire to manifest in their lives and in their being. This intended outcome will be created as a dedication for the session. You will both need to have an open mind and heart. These are most important for the transformation. It is more powerful when a vision is shared with a lover, and it will be more effective.

After establishing the vision, you will both need to let go of attachment to the outcome. You cannot plan how the session will transpire. Just be totally and unconditionally available to the receiver and support them on this journey. This could take them into rapid spiritual and personal evolution.

The intention of the giver is one of upholding, honouring, and worshipping; honouring your beloved, the whole being, and all aspects of them. The body is perceived as divine. It is the vehicle and the temple of the soul. It is through the body that divinity feels. It is through our touch that divinity touches. It is through our smell and taste that divinity perceives and experiences the manifest world.

Focusing on the image of what you desire to achieve, or your vision for your life's accomplishment, at the moments of orgasm or ejaculation is most profound and potent. Orgasm and ejaculation are the potent power of creation. Why waste a good orgasm by not dedicating it to anything or by not being aware of what you desire to achieve in your life? 'Sex magic' is the term for the conscious act of using sexuality together with vision and dedication.

In tantra, you are the beloved, you are the lover, and you are divinity itself. Rumi was a Sufi mystic. His sublime poetry encapsulates the profound experience of divine communion with the beloved, god or the universe.

VISUALIZATION

There are tantric meditations that guide you to visualize the image of your own body as a well or a fountain, where the energy is overflowing and gushing out of the crown. You become the overflowing source of abundance and bliss, allowing the river of life and the energies of the universe or nature to flow through you.

Testimonial

I truly glimpsed the power of what we are releasing together and as an individual; your experience and channelling abilities have really boosted the process in me. It is beyond pleasure and all of that, nice though it feels. The energy we have at our disposal once we have learnt how to tap in is genuinely awesome. I feel this now and realize I have the ability to use this power for the good of me and others. (B.T.)

I had a strong experience *re* manifestation, vision, and maybe even premonition. My previous experience was a jaw-dropping wow, which I didn't actually try to manifest other than in a lucid dream, but it came to pass in reality.. My god … it really did! I believe that it was as much for the benefit of the other person as me! I had a strong realization this evening that this was the tip of a big iceberg, through ritual and work together. I felt a great deal of energy in my body was enabling me to visualize something, and it was a little frightening because of the power this put in my hands. The experience was a wonderful insight into the power of the mind to make reality! (B.T.T.)

Orgasm and ejaculation are literally the potent powers of creation. You do not need an orgasm to conceive a child. Orgasm and ejaculation are actually the big bang on a human/divine scale. Why waste a good orgasm!? Use this potent power of creation prior to and during ejaculation and orgasm to manifest the very thing you desire, to help your life and for the benefit of others. Be mindful of what you think when you are ejaculating or having orgasms, 'What you think about, you bring about.' In some of the Kabbalistic and agnostic schools of thoughts, the Tree of Knowledge in the Garden of Eden is the Tree of Sexuality. In the Old Testament uses the expression 'to know' a woman; this translates to having sexual intercourse or carnal knowledge.

Some traditional Taoists hold the notion that a woman steals a man's vital force energy and that therefore men should practice non-ejaculatory sex, since ejaculation is for reproduction or rejuvenation only. However, in tantric practices, energy is circulated consciously, so there is more energy to share. In tantric practices energy is circulated consciously between the love partners, and an exchange and amplification occurs naturally, so there is more energy to share. Some Tibetan schools are more relaxed in their approach and advise to ejaculate 'only in the winter'.

Some Sufis and Kabbalists prescribe ejaculation only for a higher purpose, such as for the good of the whole community or humanity. Dedicating to world peace is an altruistic vision. Start first by changing your own life and those whom you touch, your community. Dedicating the session to your vision is sex magic. Make sure you are appearing in your vision.

It would be advisable to practice self-pleasuring daily if possible. Self-pleasuring and self-honouring is very different from masturbation. Learning to separate ejaculation from orgasm and the purpose of the self-honouring will help. In tantric self-pleasuring, I also advise dedicating to a vision.

Dedication to a vision may be used for enhancing your life, relationships, health, and work, as well as for world peace. The manifesting process using sex magic practices involves directing your raw sexual energy towards the head by focusing internally and holding the vision you desire to manifest. This could be short term goals, comprising financial benefits, projects you wish to succeed, or a long-term vision of your life

117

accomplished. It may involve having images of other people by your side, children laughing, a happy family, or communities celebrating abundance and prosperity.

You need to be in the vision, at the centre of the picture. Your life's purpose, goals, and aspirations are very individual and unique. You bring unique gifts and contributions to enhancing and evolving life on earth and the universe. You may use all the senses. This is important when practicing the sex magic manifestation ritual.

The vision needs to be communicated prior to the session commencing. You, as the giver, can remind the receiver at crucial times to conjure up and project the vision. You will help them to connect to the vision at moments of orgasm and ejaculation or at points of deciding to dedicate the vision. You can do this many times in one session. The more you practice this, and the more power you charge the vision with, the quicker the manifestation.

It is helpful to be aware that some people may have reversals and reactions to anything that can be healing and nourishing. In EFT (emotional freedom technique), the term 'psychologically reversed' describes people who do the very opposite of a suggested beneficial action. It is often observed in teenager's behaviour, but some adults may still have this tendency.

By bringing awareness to this, the person can realize they have the option to change. No one else can do it for them. It is part of the human make-up – the self-saboteur, the sabotaging parts within. Despite knowing the harm in smoking, some nurses in cancer units still take a cigarette out of a packet that is covered in horrific images and warnings.

Both partners holding a spiritual intention for the benefit of helping humanity evolve to a higher level of consciousness is one of the possible ways to dedicate the session, and it can be a starting point in a tantric healing massage. Human beings function on two main planes or levels of existence. One is the basic animalistic plane, the human animal, depicted as a horizontal plane, and the other our spiritual plane, the vertical alignment.

Humans are of both realms, and the meeting of these two planes occurs at the heart chakra. This can be illustrated as the cross. The human-animalistic plane is where you need to honour the body. You have basic needs to keep warm or cool, depending on where you reside. You need to eat, drink, urinate, and defecate. Sexual urges are all part of the human-animal basic needs.

On the other plane, the vertical alignment is the spiritual striving. Somewhere in your being you know you are of the spirit, yearning for spiritual union, knowing there is more to life than just what appears to be. That is why humanity has been striving and improving itself, and still there is more to find, learn, and experience. This yearning for wholeness, for oneness, is the fuel that drives us to explore. Our desire for spirituality is also a desire that is felt within the physical being.

Tantric Secret

Place the vision in a special place called the cave of brahma. It is not in the Himalayas as some teachers may think. It is precisely located between the occipital *medulla oblongata* where the spine enters the skull, which is the command centre and the third eye, the pineal gland, which is responsible for the serotonin levels in the body and for visions and shamanic journeying. At the very centre, if you draw a straight line from the crown, the top of your head, where it meets the diagonal line between the *medulla* and the third eye, the meeting place is the mythical cave of brahma where the whole universe opens up. There are *mudras*, gestures, and practices in the tantra *kriya yoga* that help connect and activate this powerful area.

CHAPTER 15:

Enlightenment and Self-Realization

THE CHANTING OF MANTRAS by the giver during the massage is of great importance. In most of Hindu tantra, mantras honouring and invoking the god Shiva and goddess Durga are recited. Mantras help the practitioner to tune in to the cosmic forces that make tantra a powerful tool on the path to self-actualization, or self-realization. Some spiritual teachings only encourage mantras as the vehicle of self-actualization. *Nada* yoga is a branch of yoga that focuses on mantras and sounds. See more about mantras in my Sacred Chants and in the appendix.

The safety of clear boundaries means that the receiver can relax completely into receiving the touch, without any hidden agenda from the giver. Taking our time indulging in giving and receiving the touch will enable the receiver to relax and experience states that are truly beyond description. Once you have tasted this, you **know bliss**. It is the most beautiful gift a lover can give to his or her beloved.

Love, bliss, enlightenment, clarity, oneness, and boundlessness are all words that attempt to describe the profound union with all that is. Yet the words do not reach a fraction of the profound experience. It is a state you arrive at, happening of its own accord when you let go and surrender. For Shiva the experience of brief moments of orgasms without ejaculations are the key that will let you, Shiva, into the 'Garden of Eden', discovering the well of the elixir of life and youth that is within your being.

Enjoy this amazing journey. Once you have tasted bliss, you will **know**. It is like coming home, a sense of relief at remembering who you really are, which is beyond the mind, an all-knowing state occurring within your whole being, but words cannot describe it's magnitude.

Martin Jelfs states:

> All of this was not lost from the early Christian world, and the Gospel of Thomas contains some excellent quotes such as, 'When you make the two one, and when you make the inner as the outer and the outer as the inner and the above as the below, and when you make the male and the female into a single one, so that the male will not be male and the female not be female ... then shall you enter the kingdom.

The call to be fully embodied and fully alive and fully aware is stronger than ever as our disconnection from nature – our own nature and each other's – takes its toll.

There's no enlightenment if there's no awakening in the root chakra. The question is what we do with the awakened vital life-force energy.

Testimonial

> I enjoyed very much the physical touch, but I also felt that there was spiritual contact as well, which I found very enjoyable and quite erotic. I feel quite euphoric. (A.P.)

> When the heart centre opens, poetry flows as if you embodied the greatest poets such as Rumi.

POETRY

Oh! Beloved Shakti,

> After your initiation in the cobra breath

> I feel my meditation has become more juicy and has become more intense!

Day by day I can feel your blessing you shower on me.

I really don't know how I can ever thank you for all the most precious gifts which I have received from you

Even at the time of initiation your presence and your loving guidance were taking me deeper and deeper within myself.

You were so graceful. Every time when I asked you, you replied with so much love and compassion from your heart, and your every word was so full of wisdom.

I felt your energy was so powerful, and it was really helping me to move towards my centre!

Your every teaching was so magical that even now I feel your love surrounds me!

Like a mist in the early dawn! Like a beautiful fragrance!

As the sun shines, and all the darkness is shifted!

As when **you** shine in my heart, as radiant, luminous love!

And all the darkness vanishes! Oh, I feel tremendously blissful

Having you in my Life.

Thank you, Oh Shakti. I have to say this. I have been struggling in my spiritual journey!!!

For many years. I felt that existence has blessed me so much that somehow I felt that after meeting you,

I have found my way back home.

Oh, beloved Shakti, you have entered in my life as divine Goddess,

As though I was moving in darkness and **you** out of infinite love and compassion,

Holding my hand, showed me a new way towards my spiritual journey.

With tears in my eyes, my heart feels so full of gratitude towards you

that I don't find any words. How grateful I am to you!!!

Thank you so much for entering in my life,

Guiding me towards this royal path of tantra.

I want to thank you from bottom of my heart for sharing all your knowledge and wisdom with me!

And for blessing me out of your infinite love and compassion'

Poetry by Dev. B. (one of my students)

CHAPTER 16:

The Genitals

THE FEMALE GENITALS ARE hidden in the folds of the body. Therefore, females have had to relearn how to receive sexual pleasure and honouring. Male genitals are exposed and protrude out of the body. Men are generally more familiar with how to receive pleasure, as they are touching themselves regularly throughout the day when they urinate. Men may also need to relearn how to touch in a tantric way, cultivating ejaculatory choice, allowing multiple orgasms, and learning how to prolong orgasm. If you have already mastered these, then you can skip these chapters. (To obtain a free copy of the Tantric Self-Pleasuring instruction leaflet, please contact www.tantra.uk.com or email info@tantra.uk.com.)

Despite the feminist movement and the spread of so-called sexual liberation throughout parts of the Western world, Victorian attitudes still prevail and rule our society and attitudes towards sexuality. Marketing entrepreneurs understand the power of sexuality and are harnessing it in advertisements to influence our subconscious responses, and they are able to manipulate us to buy their brands. Yet when tantra is mentioned in social events or business meetings, it is often met with juvenile responses.

Some people are ashamed of their sexuality or lack of it, and in a social setting, surrounded by their peers, they make humiliating remarks geared at making themselves look bigger. It has been forty years since the Hayward Gallery in London had an exhibition on tantra. Philip

Rawson, the curator, explained that tantra is a cosmology and a science. Cosmology is where the whole universe is mapped on the body.

The suppression of a healthy sexual appetite results in perversion and aggression. 'Healthy' does not necessarily mean what a culture or religion dictates. Some orthodox religions forbid sexual expression by their leaders or priests, yet the news seemingly often reports cases of abuse by members of the clergy, the very ones who were supposed to be the pillars of society.

Some religions are opposed to love and sexual expression by gay men and women, yet some of the people in the top hierarchy of these structures are hiding the very thing they publicly condemn – to the delight of the media once this comes to light. When we suppress or forbid the very thing we resist, we empower and give it more energy. The new age expression 'What you resist persists' can be evident and can be witnessed all around us.

Testimonial

> It feels like the effect is still 'rippling' through the body. I am very grateful for your wise, understanding, kind, and caring presence. The session felt like a solid step in the right direction in terms of the 'exorcism' of the claw (of the mother's hold). It's an exorcism through love and letting go, not through fighting it. It feels like a re-orientation to who I am. Thank you for being there. (E.V.)

William Blake wrote in 'The Marriage of Heaven and Hell':

All Bibles or sacred codes have been the causes of the following Errors:

1. That Man has two real existing principles, viz a Body and Soul.

2. That Energy called Evil is alone from the Body and that Reason called Good is alone from the Soul.

3. That God will torment Man in Eternity for following his Energies.

But the following Contraries to these are True:

1. Man has no Body distinct from his Soul for that called Body is a portion of Soul discerned by the five Senses, the chief inlets of Soul in this age.

2. Energy is the only life and is from the Body and Reason is the bound or outward circumference of Energy.

3. Energy is Eternal Delight.

Wars in the Middle East are happening between people who are sexually wounded from a very young age. Some are circumcised at eight days old, and some are circumcised at the age of ten. They are both wounded and sexually repressed. It is time to heal and make love not war. Of course there are some circumcisions that are made for health reasons, but there are many ethical issues and human rights controversies regarding these practices.

Attitudes are still behind the times where it comes to sexuality. Children should be encouraged to explore sexuality in a healthy way, and certainly their own bodies. How can a person be expected to give someone else pleasure if they do not know themselves what gives them immense pleasure? When parents are uncomfortable with their sexuality, their children pick it up emotionally and energetically. The children internalize these subliminal unconscious messages and act upon them, either in a reactive and rebellious way or by repeating the patterns.

Self-pleasuring often turns into forbidden pleasure and masturbation, which is carried out in hiding for quick relief due to social conditioning. Sexual suppression also results in obsessions and fetishism. When people attempt to determine their sexuality in black-and-white thinking, gay fantasies can become an issue. The belief that we all are or have the ability to be bisexual and that it is simply a preference and a choice is very liberating. Then you can just relax into real contact with people without rejecting or objecting and expending vital energy on determining what sexual pigeonhole you fit into.

Testimonial

> At the same time I could also feel the contracted pain in the belly intensifying, feeling somewhat threatened by and resistant to this openness to life and love. I now know that this claw isn't just my mother but that it is an accumulation of all the conditioning of my upbringing. (E.V.)

Three Conscious Ways to Touch the Genitals

It is important that we learn to claim our raw sexual energy and to familiarize ourselves with pleasure and bliss. There are three ways to touch our own genitals.

Masturbation

The sole intention of this touch is to create a release. It is a form of relief, to help us with stress, even with sleep. It can be a form of addiction that could deplete men of their life-force energy. Masturbation is different for men and women. We offer different exercises for men and women in our work as psycho-sexual therapists.

Self-Pleasuring

This is a way to enjoy the body and self-touch, amplifying the orgasmic energy in the body and spreading it all over the body so it is not concentrated just in the genital areas. Ejaculation may or may not be the result, but the wonderful feeling of deep fulfilment is achieved.

For a free hand-out on how to do tantric self-pleasuring, contact www.tantra.uk.com or email info@tantra.uk.com

Self-Honouring

This is where you touch as if you are touching the body of the divine. Touch yourself as if the beloved is touching you – as if the whole universe is making love to your whole being. Genitals are not excluded, but the whole body can be in an orgasmic bliss state. To glimpse what can be experienced, read poetry by Rumi, Kabir, Hafis, and Lilith and the songs of Solomon. The mantra *Aum Ahadi Aum* is a profound practice cultivating this feeling of touching the divine and being at one with all that is.

SEVEN RS OF SEX

Sex is divine and exquisite; nothing would exist in our world if it was not due to sex:

1. reproduction

2. relaxation

3. recreational

4. relational

5. regenerational

6. religious

7. remembrance of transcendence

In Latin *sexus* means division. In tantra we refer to sexual act as 'love union'. Making love literally describes what occurs during or after the act of union.

THE LOVE MUSCLES

Your pelvic floor muscles are the pubo-coccygeal muscles, also known as the 'PC pumps'. These are the tantric muscles. They span from the pubic bone to the coccyx. There are three main sets of muscles – the pubic area, the genital area, and the perineum and anus. For both men and women they can be strengthened through Kegel exercises. Most women are made aware that after childbirth they need to exercise their pelvic floor muscles. It is also important for men to exercise these muscles regularly.

When you first start to work with them, you may not feel any difference. However, as you practice more, you will begin to feel them and identify between the different sets of muscles and different parts of your genitals. The whole of the body is mapped in the genitals and is connected with energy lines.

By exercising your PC muscles, they will charge you like a magnet; in yoga this is called the *moola bhanda* or root lock. This is a spiritual lock transmuting raw sexual energy up in the central channel, the *shushumna*, and supercharging your energy. This will create an effect like a magnet, attracting what you desire. You will benefit from practicing and stimulating these muscles daily to achieve results. It is very important to develop these muscles for the reasons described in the following section.

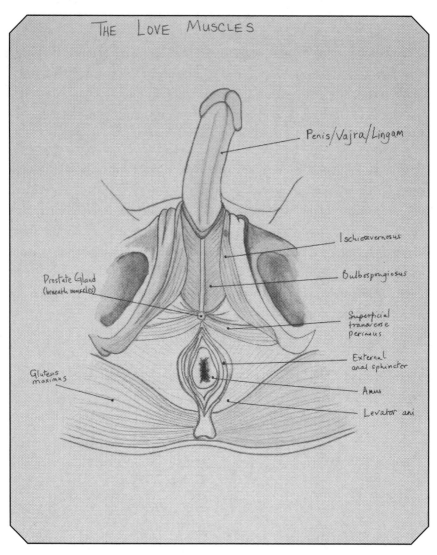

Image 26: Male Pelvic Floor Muscles (1)

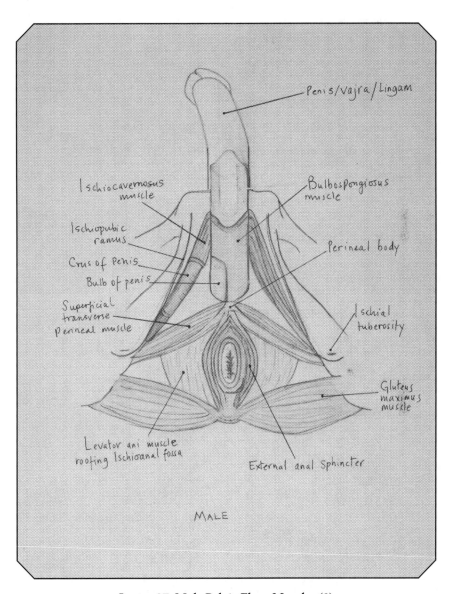

Image 27: Male Pelvic Floor Muscles (2)

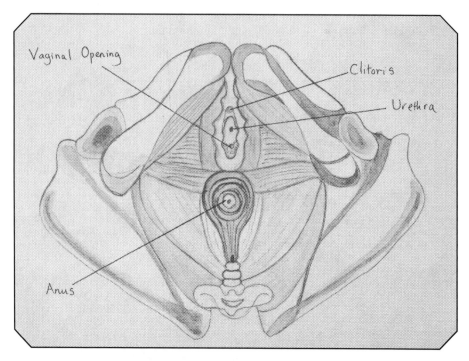

Image 28: Female Pelvic Floor Muscles

EIGHT BENEFITS OF EXERCISING YOUR LOVE MUSCLES

1. (Men) It will help create and maintain erection.

2. (Men) It will help ejaculation control and mastery of ejaculatory choice.

3. (Both men and women) The strength of your PC muscles will determine the strength of your physical orgasm. The physical orgasm is a contraction of these muscles. Some can bring about an orgasm by simply contracting them at will.

4. (Both men and women) It will eliminate incontinence later on in life. All men and women with age will become incontinent if they don't use these muscles.

5. (Men) It helps prevent prostate cancer. (See Gateway to Heaven section below.)

6. (Both men and women) These are included in the core muscles used in Feldenkrais, Alexander technique and pilates for promoting health.

7. (Both men and women) It makes you energetically attractive and helps you supercharge the *shushumna*, the central channel; you become a magnet attracting what you desire or focus on.

8. (Both men and women) The *moola bandha* is the root lock, propelling the spiritual enlightenment process as well as vitality.

Testimonial

This has changed my life. It made me realize that my relationship was not about pure sexuality but mostly about sensuality. During Hanna's workshops I started to explore my own body and became aware of the power of the senses. It gave depth to my marriage and improved my self-esteem dramatically. (P.K.)

CHAPTER 17:

The Gateway to Heaven

MALE PROSTATE MASSAGE AND THE MALE K.A.G. SPOTS

THE TANTRIC NAME FOR the anus is the gateway to heaven or the rosetta. The rosetta (anus) massage including the male prostate and the male K. A. and G. spots, could help in the following areas:

Facilitating becoming a multi-orgasmic man

Experiencing extended massive orgasm

Helping prevent prostate cancer

Riding the waves of bliss

Harnessing sexual charge and orgasms

Experiencing the orgasmic plateau, erotic trance

The gateway to heaven massage is one of the most incredibly exquisite erotic ways in which a man could have a connection with divinity and experience multiple orgasms. It literally feels as if it is a doorway to heaven, and it can be enormously healing on many levels. Some clients report that 'it is better than sex.' A man can experience the depth of multiple orgasms and connect to his K, A, and G 'spots', something they have never imagined possible.

The male G spot, also known as the sacred spot, would be more correctly referred to as the male G gland or P gland. The G spot region is the prostate gland. It can be stimulated externally by pressing in the perineum, where you can feel an indentation, a hollow, as you press quite firmly with sufficient pressure to produce a pleasurable 'Ahh' from the receiver. These muscles are very strong. You can apply more pressure than you may think possible, and it feels divine. The male sacred spot can also be stimulated inside the anus.

Stimulating the prostate gland could create a healing effect, helping in the prevention of prostate cancer.

Stimulating this area can sometimes cause an initial sensation of needing to eliminate or the urge to ejaculate. However, this can be overcome, and there is then an immense pleasure experienced.

The way to facilitate a tantric prostate massage is with great care and honouring. It is a great privilege when you are giving or receiving a sacred spot massage. It is also an incredible feeling to have your beloved giving you unconditional love and timeless honouring. Receiving their trust and vulnerability and sharing such profound erotic states with you will stay with them for a long time and may move them emotionally.

In some individuals it may take several attempts to gradually build trust and enable them to let go and surrender to the new sensations in the body that may go against the grain of cultural conditioning and perceptions. It could be challenging emotionally and mentally, as some of the areas directly stimulated are located inside the rectum. The anus is often mistakenly perceived by many as a dirty area. This is a huge misconception, as often the anus has fewer bacteria than the amount found in and around the mouth.

Heterosexual men are not supposed to enjoy anal penetration. However, all men, heterosexual, gay, and bi, have the G, the K, and the A spot. These are meant to be pleasurable and are not exclusive to gay men. Some men may be concerned that if they enjoy anal stimulation this may mean they are gay. It is very simple to determine whether your prostate is gay or not. The writer Deborah Sundhal, said, 'If you are gay, your prostate is also gay. If you are heterosexual, then your prostate is heterosexual.' I say that if you are bi, then you are very fortunate.

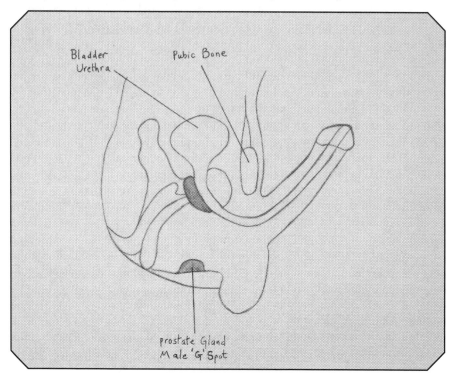

Bladder
Urethra
Pubic Bone

prostate Gland
Male 'G' Spot

Image 29: The Male G Spot

Testimonial

It felt like the most fantastic journey that a being could ever take, my Gateway to Bliss, a place I knew felt good, but could never imagine the ultimate bliss that it could produce! I have so much to learn ... Connection with the divine – to experience True Bliss - to be at one with all. (J.)

> I believe this 'liberation' is demonstrably winning back for men an important part of the masculine nature that our society has corrupted for its own selfish ends. I believe this change of mind occurred purely as a result of me noticing it in a non-judgmental way ... What a powerful thing! My body is rejuvenated, my

spine still warm from the kundalini energy, my gateway aroused and receptive for more! I lost track of time, but I would imagine that I was in a state of orgasmic pleasure for over an hour. The feeling of intense orgasm never really left me during the session – so expertly facilitated. The orgasms that were pulsing through my whole body took me to a place that was **everywhere** and **nowhere** at the same time. I do feel as though I have been opened up to a healthier way of thinking and feeling and behaving. (B.D.)

THE THREE KEY AREAS, K., A., AND G.

For both men and women, there are three key areas, the K spot, the A Spot, and the G spot.

The K spot is the *kunda* point at the inside of the end of the coccyx, the tailbone. This point can awaken kundalini. When you are honouring heaven's gate, the receiver is lying on their front, inserting the finger slightly curved upwards to touch the coccyx, it will activate the *kunda* point. It is an esoteric, energetic spot and it can feel as if a matchstick has been ignited. It is the end of the tail of the 'snake'. If the receiver is lying on their back, the finger will be curved downwards.

The A spot is the crown point in a man or the anterior fornix erogenous zone in a woman, also known as the AFEZ. You can activate this area by pointing the finger inside the anus straight towards the crown. In women it is found at the entrance to the cervix, located where the anterior walls of the vagina begin to curve. In a man it is found inside his anus, directly pointing a straight finger towards the top of the head; the exact location will vary according to the internal organ and the finger length.

As it is mainly an energetic point, the man will be able to feel it, even if your finger does not reach deep. Sometimes doing this massage energetically only, can produce phenomenal results without even inserting a finger.

Tapping upwards or down will simulate both parts of the A spot on the uterus wall or the posterior wall in the anus. There are theories that the AFEZ is a degenerated female prostate which are also attributed to the female G spot and the Skene's gland, the lesser vestibular glands.

The male G spot can be activated both from outside in the perineum or internally inserting the finger curved as if you are beckoning as mentioned before.

If it has been agreed that this will be included in the session, then explain at the beginning of the session, before any touch commences, how this will be performed. Stress that the receiver has the say and the ultimate control at any point over what occurs in the session. It is certainly not like a medical examination, and some doctors go to tantric practitioners to have the sacred spot massaged. When working with clients, make sure you have experienced a whole course in receiving and giving under supervision, so you know what it can feel like and also what can arise emotionally. Every time you receive an anal massage, different sensations and feelings may be experienced. Reading about it or watching it is not sufficient for attaining a level of competence.

Often when this is the first time a heterosexual man experiences the honouring around the gateway to heaven, he may be preoccupied with many stories from his conditioning. At times you can observe the hands as they will give clues if any internal conflicts arise within your partner. Their hands may clench in fear or tetany reaction, or they may be expressing pleasure and even replicating the movements. You can assess their receptiveness and the level of enjoyment as you use long strokes, connecting touch via the rectum entrance from the sacrum to the inner thighs. It is better to have them wanting your touch and being aroused, if erotic energy and enjoyment is the intention. Brushing your hands across the whole of the length from the inner thighs, past the anus, and up to the middle back will help them relax into this new sensation.

In sacred spot healing (G spot for both men and women), where emotional and physical issues are present, it can work on both energetic and physical levels. The receiver does not need to be consciously aware of what is being released in order for healing to occur. Sacred-spot work could bring to the surface suppressed issues and traumas ready to be released and dispersed energetically.

Testimonial

> A totally wonderful and positive experience. I went in feeling shaky, tearful, vulnerable, inadequate, and confused. I came out feeling elated, full of energy, optimistic, and with a clear sense of my own worth. The experience was cathartic. Something that was not serving me had somehow been 'flushed out' in a way I still don't understand and certainly don't need to. The high energy, optimism, and sense of my own worth stayed with me for days afterwards. It is wonderful to know that this healing experience is available to me, as and when I feel the need. What was delivered to me was much more than most of us would understand by 'massage'. Truthfully, I cannot think of a better way of describing it, except to say that for me it was a deep healing experience, which delivered amazing benefits to me. (A.S.)

The external prostate spot is also known as the '100-million-dollar spot'. It's the point on the perineum near the anus that is like a slight impression or a dip, a cave-like indentation as you apply pressure. Start with slight pressure, as this can be sensitive depending on sexual history and general prostate health. Stimulating this point helps to eliminate the need to ejaculate and can create the experience in men called the valley orgasm. This is when you relax into orgasm. It is the opposite of tensing in an orgasm.

The valley orgasm is an orgasm that is very different, felt much deeper in the body and also all over the body. This can be achieved by surrendering and relaxing. It can last much longer than any 'conventional' orgasm without experiencing the loss of semen and resulting in prolonged states of sexual pleasure. During internal prostate massage, moving the finger on his left side inside the anus will stimulate his feminine and intuitive aspect, moving on his right side will stimulate his masculine side, cognitive, linear thinking. It is wonderful to stroke an arc starting from the left to the right slowly. This will harmonize his masculine and feminine aspects and at the same time he could have profound sexual orgasmic pleasure. This can also be applied to the female yoni, vulva.

To stress again, always seek for an actual verbal confirmation prior to inserting a finger inside the body. 'May I insert my finger?' or 'Would you like me to move my finger inside you now?' or 'Would you like to have my finger inside?' or similar. Ask a direct question and do not proceed until you get a clear verbal 'yes'. Also check for an energetic 'yes' and the body communication of a 'yes'. During the contractual agreement prior to the massage commencing, you would have received consent, otherwise you would not have contemplated venturing to the gateway to heaven.

Once you have received all the four consents (verbal consent during the orientation talk, energetic consent, body response, and verbal consent just before carrying out sacred spot honouring), you place a finger at the entrance of the gateway to heaven. Invite them to take your finger in. Ask them, 'Would you please take my finger in?' or 'Would you please draw my finger in using your pelvic floor muscles?' Encourage them to move their body and particularly the pelvis to take your finger in at their own pace. Be still and attuned to their breathing and any other signs of changes in their being and responses.

There are two major sets of sphincter muscle rings. One set is voluntary, which you have total control over. The other set is involuntary, and you have no conscious control over them, just as your blood pumps and flows in your body without you having to do any conscious action to help the process.

Before removing the finger, make sure you always inform the receiver and ask for an actual verbal confirmation, 'May I take my finger out?' or 'Would it be okay to remove my finger now?' If the response is 'yes', then proceed to invite the receiver with the question, 'Would you please exhale my finger out?' Shiva, the man god, may take several breaths. On exhaling and relaxing, the finger will gradually be expelled and pushed out at its own pace. Make sure that after the finger has been expelled, you cup the hand over the gateway to heaven so that the receiver will not feel abandoned.

When entering the gateway to heaven, the rectum, if Shiva is too tight to be able to allow you to move inside his body comfortably, invite him to kneel with his head lower than his pelvis, enabling the supercharged energy to flow to his head on the ground or the massage surface. Press into his occipital, towards the *medulla oblongata* where the spine enters the skull, to encourage the energy to flow, thus opening up the whole area and the *shushumna*, the central channel. You can also penetrate him energetically. For some people it feels physically strong, and they are surprised afterwards when they realize no physical penetration took place. This is also used in healing for women in cases such as vaginismus.

Invite him to laugh or to make noise while exhaling audibly. This will help open the two sphincter muscle rings. Clenching and relaxing the PC muscles will result in pumping blood and will stimulate the prostate. This will benefit all men in various ways as mentioned in the Eight Benefits section earlier.

All men after the age of seventy are susceptible to contracting prostate cancer if they do not stimulate and pay attention to their prostate. Some doctors recommend stimulation of the prostate for cancer prevention, and some recommend it for healing cancers. You will be advised to seek professional doctor's advice and conventional allopathic medical treatments, as well as using complementary therapies of your own choosing. As mentioned earlier, the book *Prostate Health in 90 days Without Surgery or Intervention* by Larry Clapp is highly recommended for both men and women.

The anus and internal anal stimulation can also be a very profound place for women, though in a slightly different way, since the female G spot is located inside her yoni or vagina. The female G spot and A spot could be activated from within the anus through the vaginal walls. Certainly the K spot (the anterior point of the coccyx) will be activated and awakened, which is an extraordinary experience for a woman. It is done by still holding, touching, or pointing towards the K spot, and just being present. Allow the energy to build up by being totally still, and then as the K spot is activated, it may feel as if a matchstick is ignited. Orgasms may start lapping at the shore of her being. Some women prefer to have the K spot activated while they are lying on their back. Some also prefer to have their yoni held inside. They feel more fulfilled, and a physical and emotional satiation level is attained.

Testimonials

Tantric massage was one of the best experiences of my life. I attained a transcendent state of celestial joy, a feeling of connecting to all aspects of the self: child and adult, male and female, moving into the spirit. I was in a relatively speechless state for hours afterwards, just processing what I had learnt. *Tantra does not mean sex here – it is clearly the real thing!* (D.J.)

> A wonderful and intense experience. I felt a complete sense of calmness and wellbeing. The orgasms were the most intense and as spectacular as I could imagine, encompassing my entire body and being. I truly felt total unity with the universe and felt at the very centre of it, strength through serenity. Even now I still feel the warmth and energy. (R.C.D.M)

CHAPTER 18:

Honouring the Female Yoniverse

THE VAGINA, THE YONIVERSE

THE VAGINA IS THE yoni, meaning the sacred place or tomb, the sacred source of all, the 'yoni-verse'. The whole universe and its mysteries are held at a woman's sacred place. Your vulva is so unique, like your face, or your being. There is no other like yours. Like a snowflake or a flower, each is so precious and beautiful. I refer to the yoni as divine design.

Men are in awe and can be in fear of the power, the magic, and the pleasures it offers beyond description. It gives life and also is the tomb where men('s ego) could die during an orgasm – *le petit mort*, the little death.

There is an ancient tantric teaching that says men become enlightened when they meditate on the yoni, the female genital. Meditating on the yoni for both will create healing and reconnection to their true nature. When a lover surrenders to the yoni's mysteries and allows himself to dive deeply into the sacred place in devotion to the woman goddess, then as a devotee he loses himself and is said to be reborn as a god or a goddess.

Yoni *pujas* or rituals are still practiced in various forms. The inner form, as it is commonly practiced, is a meditation on an image or a statue representing the yoni. This might consist of making an offering of devotion (*prasad*), a divine gift – anointing the statue of Devi or a yoni with offerings of milk, feathers, and incense representing the element of air, with yoghurt, a conch-shell, or flowers representing earth, with honey representing the element of fire, or with water and oil representing ether. This *puja* can also be in the form of a secret ritual, where the worship of a yoni is carried out in the embodiment of a living goddess and may be a physical penetration in honouring her yoni. The love fluids produced are regarded as highly potent and are used for initiation and honouring rituals, as well as ingesting. A menstruating goddess is regarded as highly potent and revered.

Thanks to the sixties and seventies sexual revolution and women's liberation movement, women regained equal rights, though at the same time they gave up their femininity. Most women work very hard at trying to be the same as men, and in the process they emasculate them. A lot of women need to relearn how to get in touch with their femininity, just as men go to workshops and lodges to reconnect with their masculinity.

Much damage has been done by to the fashion of 'designer vagina', a trend of voluntary genital mutilation, cutting away the most sensitive parts of their being, the labia.

Hildegard of Bingen, a twelfth-century female mystic and sage, was known to be in total devotional and ecstatic union with the divine and the Christ. She is still famous for the extraordinary sublime celestial music she composed and for her paintings. This famous painting of hers is used for Christmas cards. It depicts the yoniverse. It clearly shows the clitoral hood as the moon, the labia, the urethra, and the entrance to the yoni, the vulva. It also shows the hymen and the gateway to heaven, which is the rosetta, the anus.

Image 30: Yoniverse, Twelfth-Century Painting by Hildegard of Bingen

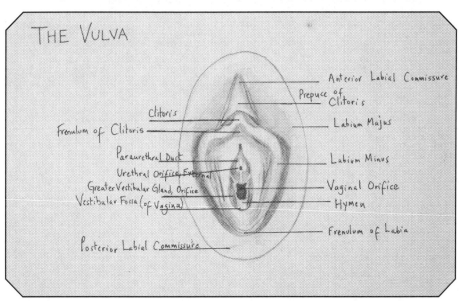

Image 31: Yoni, the Vulva

A superb three-dimensional model of the female genital anatomy can be found at www.3Dvulva.com.

To approach the most sacred place of a woman, you need to be patient and prepare the woman goddess to receive your touch at her inner sanctum. Starting from the inner thighs, inscribe a triangle beginning at a point on the inside of her knee, then moving to the base of her yoni by the groin, the crease in the thigh, and the edge of the buttocks. There are lymph nodes there. It is best to start with her left side, which is her feminine and receptive side. This could be highly erotic, and she may enjoy receiving in this area in preparation. It will also help send her onto the orgasmic plane. This area includes the psoas muscles, a tantric erogenous zone on the thigh and groin. Explore and allow plenty of time. Make note in which areas you get responses, and notice any subtle changes in her breathing as clues.

Women are also responsible for their own orgasm. If they do not move or use breath and sound or participate in the process, they cannot expect their partner to 'give' them an orgasm. An orgasm is about letting go; it will then take over and wash through their whole being.

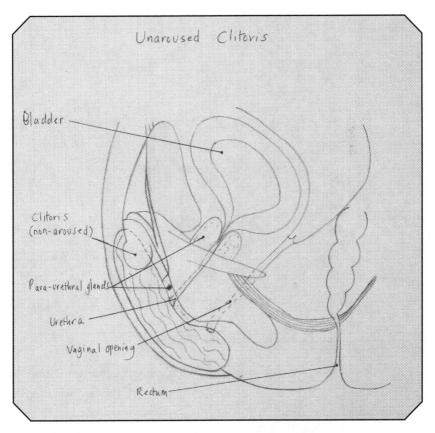

Image 32: Unaroused Clitoris

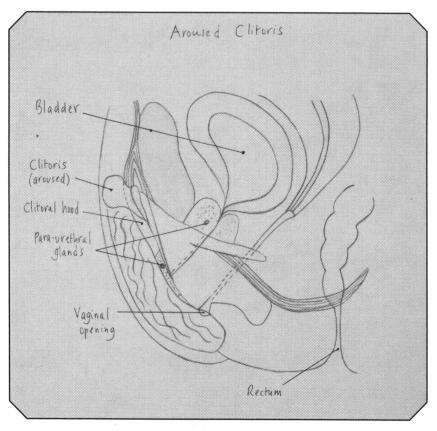

Image 33: Aroused Clitoris

DEMYSTIFYING THE FEMALE G 'SPOT'

The female G 'spot' would be better honoured with the name female G gland or the female prostate gland or the G zone. The female prostate gland is the whole gland that can engorge when the woman is aroused. It spans from surrounding the clitoris and includes the opening of the urethra and the vaginal opening, all the way inside the vagina and behind the pubic bone to the G spot. The area that is commonly referred to as the female G spot is an area that will only become apparent to both the giver and receiver when the woman is sexually aroused. The spot becomes engorged, swells, and becomes prominent as it pushes the tissue and the vaginal wall; it grows to approximately the size of a walnut. It is located behind the pubic bone and can be reached deep inside her by inserting one or two fingers, curved with a beckoning gesture as if you are motioning 'come here.'

This can be an elusive zone when a woman disconnects and disowns her sexuality and her power due to trauma. The healing can be activated by reconnecting to this area and activating her G zone. When a woman is aroused the G spot will engorge and be detectable physically. It is fascinating how science is now able to provide scientific proof of these teachings and the knowledge that tantrics and yogis have been practicing for many centuries. For example, the existence of the female G spot has only been accepted relatively recently in the modern medical books. Now there is the 'new discovery' of the male G spot, even though it has been there for thousands of years.

The female prostate gland, which was overlooked for centuries, is profoundly important in facilitating and giving sexual pleasure as well in as healing. In the late nineteenth and early twentieth centuries, doctors used to 'administer' treatment to women suffering from 'hysteria', and 'pelvic congestion' was the symptom. Highly respected doctors, to 'alleviate pelvic congestion', used, apart from their hand, special tools, early version of vibrators. Some were mechanically operated, some were filled with water, and others operated by electricity. These are on display in sex museums around the world.

Women overlook this important gland due to miseducation about exploring their sexuality. In some medical text books, there is still misinformation about the female sexual anatomy, even to the extent of total omission, though this is changing fast. In some Muslim and African cultures, the barbaric inhuman practice of female circumcision – mutilating the genitals and cutting off the clitoris – is still practiced. Some of these brave women have had to learn to take their pleasure into their own hands and have learned other ways to bring pleasure and honouring. The customs of women in some of these cultures are highly supportive of each other; they spend time together, nourishing and healing themselves. Even though more healing is needed, it is a step in the right direction to empowering themselves. Gay or lesbian activities have been an accepted practice in these cultures for centuries, though not overtly.

Other factors that have contributed to the trauma stored in the genitals include poor sexual habits and using nonadjustable high-speed low-quality non-silicon sex toys. Unsatisfactory sexual acts that are not honouring the female genitals are a form of abuse. All these could have contributed to numbing of the potentially highly sensitive and sexually arousing female prostate gland. The answer to this is to regain sensitivity in the genitals, to honour your genitals. Explore and learn about your body. It would be so healing, healthy, and honouring if all women learned to love their genitals. Use a magnifying mirror to explore yourself to learn about your beautiful vagina. Draw her, and learn to love the unique shape of the petals, the labia. Learn to like your own smell and taste. Your unique smell is what arouses your partner, not the manufactured perfumes we use to mask our real smell.

DE-MYSTIFYING FEMALE EJACULATION

At present few women are aware that they have the capacity to ejaculate. This phenomenon is revolutionary in this age in some cultures, although it is depicted in ancient tantric art. Some Taoist pictures show tantric masters collecting the female ejaculate in a cup.

Image 34: Female Ejaculation, Old Taoist Print

Sex education at schools has some catching up to do. The good news is that all women have the capacity to ejaculate. Sometimes women can ejaculate without even knowing what is happening. It may occur as additional moistness or sudden wetness.

Female ejaculation appears in the Bible at various times. The twenty-first century tantric writer Moses in his article about the bible and female ejaculatory orgasms wrote:

> Nahmanides was a Jewish mystic, writing a marriage manual for the Cabbala. Its purpose was to produce learned sons. What impressed me most as a Protestant—I protest everything—was the Hebrew translation of Leviticus 12:2: "When a woman has an emission…" This is the first reference to female ejaculatory orgasms in Western Literature! … Leviticus is attributed to Moses (1425 BCE) and thought by some to first be transcribed from the oral tradition by Ezra around 1000 BCE. … It was around 400 BCE when Hippocrates came up with the "double seed" theory. This said male ejaculate and female ejaculate each contained seeds needed for conception of a child. … Galen (200 CE) confirmed this. The Roman Church from its inception in 325 CE promoted female ejaculatory orgasm for purposes of procreation until 1770. (http://thesacredfemale.wordpress.com/2011/06/09/the-bible-and-female-ejaculatory-orgasms/)

Some women ejaculate a vast quantity. This features in some porn movies where it is referred to as 'squirting'. The porn industry regards this ability as if it is a goal to attain. This may make some women feel inadequate and have a sense of failure. Some women may have experienced wet dreams. Many think they have wet themselves by mistake, by passing a pure, clear fluid. Female ejaculate is very different from urine in its texture, viscosity, smell, taste, and colour. The viscosity can be silky watery in texture and has no odour, though sometimes a sweet scent can be detected. It is certainly not the same as urine. This is the highly prized female ejaculate.

Prior to the honouring massage session commencing, a woman should empty her bladder. Then if the receiving female partner feels as if she wants to urinate, you will know that this is more likely to be female ejaculation. Encourage her to stay with these new sensations and let go. Ensuring she has plenty of towels beneath her will help. Toilet training and 'proper' behaviour have contributed to the sexual ignorance and judgmental imprinting that women have internalized. This, of course, affects their ability to let go into orgasms and will hinder the experience of female ejaculation. Nowadays there are under-sheet bed covers that are wonderful for such practice. Make sure they are high quality under-sheet covers; it makes a difference in smell, feel, and hygiene.

In yoga, the *ojas*, the life force energy juices, are present in the female and male ejaculation. These are highly potent and nourishing. They are the much sought after elixir of life and youth!

As mentioned before, there is a secret tantric practice where the practitioners collect the *ojas*, the highly prized elixir of life and rejuvenation. There are two ways to 'collect' or accumulate these highly charged potent energies. One way is by sublimation within the body, where the practitioner takes the energy and redirects it inside and to the love partner without any liquid coming out of the body, though they can both taste and smell the sweetness of the *amrita*. This is the hidden or the subtle practice. The other way is to capture and use the *amrita*. You can capture the *ojas* in a chalice or a cup and use it in a secret tantric meditation as an offering in the cup ceremony.

To learn the procedure and see illustrations of this, see the massage ritual sequence later on in the book or on the DVDs available from www.tantra.uk.com or by email info@tantra.uk.com

Explore your vagina or your beloved's. Have a good look and locate your urethra, the small opening below the clitoris where the female ejaculation will appear. Allow yourself to enjoy the feelings and the arousal. At some point of arousal you may naturally produce more lubrication. Notice where this liquid originates; it comes from the urethra.

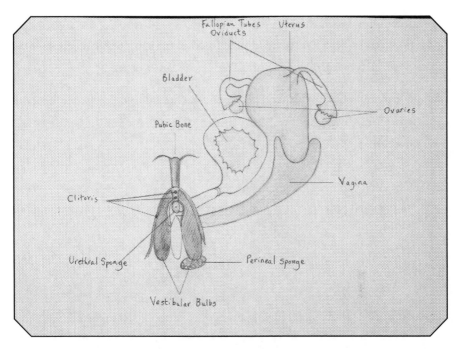

Image 35: Female Reproductive System

When you are in the midst of sexual arousal, just stay with this and then at a point of a high arousal or when you feel an orgasm coming, bearing down, push with all your might. Have plenty of towels below and really allow yourself to let go.

It is one of the most liberating moments, where the shackles of fears and inhibitions are pierced through. At that very moment they disperse, leaving you floating in oceanic bliss. The bliss will descend upon you, and you can carry on riding these orgasmic waves of bliss as you enter a new realm, experiencing female ejaculation.

When you have your partner's fingers inside, or in sexual union, where the woman is positioned mounting her lover, she can push down with her vaginal muscles, as if giving birth or defecating. Explore this new way and the new sensations.

Often women go to the toilet to urinate and disperse the *ojas*, the potent sexual juices, in the middle of a love-making session or tantric massage. Often it is the female ejaculation and not urine.

Make sure when honouring the yoni, you use plenty of water-based lubricant or a high quality raw (not extracted by boiling) organic coconut oil.

CHAPTER 19:
The Brain and the Occiput

THE PRIMARY BRAIN

OUR PRIMARY BRAIN IS our largest erotic organ. It translates, interprets, and anticipates scenarios. The brain is so powerful, and we currently understand only a fraction of it. It weighs approximately three pounds, less than a kilo and a half.

At a certain period of human life, while the woman is fertile and the man is potent, the brain is constantly on the lookout for opportunities for mating. Sex really matters and affects every aspect of our life, even though we may not like to admit it publicly.

The brain is a chemical manufacturer and will excrete and flood the body with natural opiates such as dopamine, endorphins, prolactin, oxytocin, serotonin and vasopressin. These help us get into the mood, relax and enhance our sexual appetite and performance or endurance.

The Main Parts of the Brain

1. **The reptilian brain** is the cerebellum, the little brain, the parietal lobe, the brain stem, which is concerned with survival and primitive responses. It is operating at a pre-personal level. It is located below the first part and in front of the second. It is associated with controlling balance and coordination, movement, orientation, recognition, perception of stimuli, posture, and balance. It connects

155

the spinal cord to the brain. It controls involuntary and automatic processes regulating heart rate, blood pressure, breathing, and digestion

2. **The midbrain** is associated with our senses and is concerned with personal development and our ego structure. The temporal lobe or the frontal lobe is concerned with movement, feeling, thinking and reasoning, the ability to solve problems, planning, parts of speech, auditory stimuli, memory, perception and recognition.

3. The third part of the brain is associated with the transpersonal level of our evolution, where we can perceive the benefit for all humanity, where we experience oneness, unity consciousness. This part of the brain includes **the occipital lobe**, which is associated with visual processing. This is only found in mammals, associated with 'higher' information processing by more fully evolved animals such as humans, primates, and dolphins.

4. **The limbic system**: the emotional brain, is found buried within the cerebrum. This system contains the thalamus, hypothalamus, amygdala, and hippocampus. When we have a repetitive thought, the Hypothalamus creates neuropeptides that are translated into feelings and addictions.

5. **The right hemisphere** of the brain will be lighting up when bliss states, ecstasy, and sexual activity are experienced. This is the emotional part of the brain

6. **The left frontal lobe** is activated when you experience pleasure.

7. **The left side of the brain**, the cognitive, will light up when thoughts about love or a lover are experienced.

8. **The left pre-frontal cortex** is associated with happiness. The left forebrain, anterior insula, and pre-central gyrus

activate by pleasure. Meditation is a measured method to activate the pleasure and happiness centres in the brain.

Oxytocin

Oxytocin, the cuddle-and-trust hormone is released when we feel amorous or affectionate. It is referred to as the love molecule, helping intimacy and strengthening social relationships and attachments. It is freely available anywhere: simply shake hands, think of someone you love dearly, caress and hug another or a pet. It also works through looking lovingly with your eyes. Oxytocin helps alleviate anxiety and stress and breakdown social divisions. It increases self-esteem, a sense of optimism, generosity, and selfless acts, which is what makes us human.

The combination of oxytocin, dopamine, and norepinephrine, is a crucial ingredient in forging couple bonding. It increases desire and sexual arousal and will help maintain male erections. Sexual arousal registers the highest levels of oxytocin, which is likely to result in an orgasm. For women during an orgasm oxytocin floods the brain, later resulting in the desire to cuddle and bond. It also helps women induce labour (in the form of the drug Piocin), contracting the uterus. After childbirth it is responsible for the bonding between mother and baby by touch and eye-gazing. Oxytocin helps in pain management, healing wounds, and postpartum, after childbirth, it acts as anti-depressant.

Human emotions, such as anger, irritation, and happiness, are the result of a chemical reaction on a cellular level that we are so familiar with and may be addicted to. The neurons (nerve cells in the brain) create a network that originates from a repetitive thought or a strong memory, re-enacting it and connecting in the mind to current situations, which reinforces the feelings. The hypothalamus creates chemicals that are unique to each emotion. These chemicals are called peptides, small clusters of amino acid chains called neurohormones or neuropeptides. These neuropeptides produce different chemicals for fear, joy, anger, and happiness. As soon as an emotion is activated, the hypothalamus creates peptides and releases them via the pituitary gland into the blood stream, which is then distributed to all parts of the body. When this is activated, often the body needs its regular chemical injection which is triggered by a particular emotion which is part of the emotional addiction.

The sense of self is experienced as awareness, the witness consciousness, or the internalized observer. This is sometimes experienced as a continual commentary or at time experienced as an internal critical monolog. Both hemispheres of the brain are engaged in this activity.

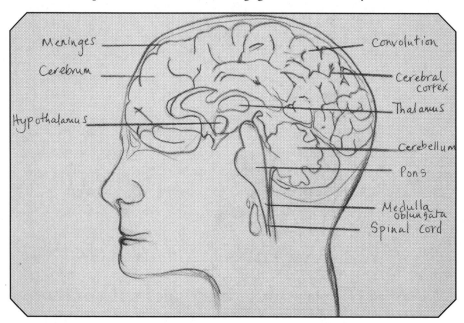

Image 36: Brain Anatomy

We find relief in losing our sense of self, or a place of no-mind, when we experience deep intimacy or profound orgasm or ecstatic spiritual union. Some find it through food or drugs and alcohol, others through meditations or hypnosis. Some seek it to their detriment and overdose. DMT (dimethyltryptamine) is a hallucinogenic plant-based compound, a psychedelic tryptamine which is used for shamanic journeying in indigenous cultures. The same effect can be achieved by the chemicals created by the brain. Often the yoga practice of *kechari mudra* can induce such experience.

Letting go of identification with who we are or our stories, dissolving the boundaries of the physical body, we can experience a sense of oneness, tasting or touching bliss. It is a visceral, felt phenomenon.

SECOND AND THIRD BRAIN

The heart centre is the 'second brain' from which the body wisdom and emotional intelligence stem.

The 'third brain' is in the gut. There are about a hundred million serotonin neurons in this area, far more than in the spinal cord and the peripheral nervous system. The third brain spans from the oesophagus in the neck all the way to the rectum. It is sometimes referred to as the enteric brain.

THE MEDULLA OBLONGATA AND THE OCCIPUT

The medulla oblongata is located inside the head and is a region of the brain. It is also the command centre that enables us to carry out voluntary and involuntary functions. The occipital or the occiput is the bony base of the skull where the spine enters the skull. This point is the most important point during the massage.

When we awaken the latent kundalini energy to come out of its dormant place, coiled and nestled in the sacrum at the base of the spine, we direct it towards the medulla. Esoterically, we are directing Shakti kundalini, raw sexual energy, upwards to turn it into more Shiva consciousness, or awareness.

Tantric Secret

By stimulating and pressing into the occiput, the third eye and the top of the crown chakra, the cave of brahma is activated. The cave of brahma is in the physical gap between the two brain hemispheres that goes from the third eye to the occiput. It is halfway on the diagonal line between the two. It is also stimulated by putting the tip of your tongue up to the roof of

159

your mouth. *Kechari mudra* is a practice in yoga, placing the tongue in specific locations inside the mouth to activate various glands.

KETCHARI MUDRA, MEDULLA, PITUITARY AND PENIAL GLANDS

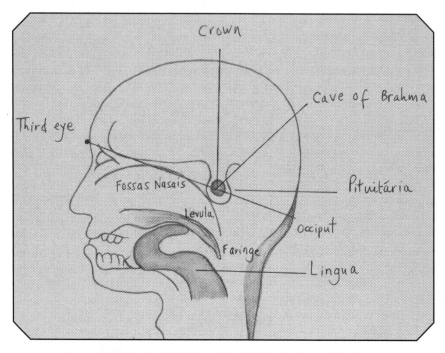

Image 37: *Ketchari Mudra*, Pineal Gland, Cave of Brahma

The cave of brahma is your esoteric manifesting point, the place of connection to the whole universe; there are no limits here. This place is where you can plug into and access universal knowledge and experiences, where the whole universe opens up. When the cave of brahma is activated, you can experience a deep sense of knowing. Some have a 'downloading' experience, where they receive information and cannot explain its origins. Some call it channelling the 'akashic records', mystical knowledge that is in the ethers. Some people are said to have channelled information and some painted while asleep.

When we drop into a state of deep sleep, reaching delta brain waves, or state of *turia*, that is where we connect with bliss and akasha, all knowledge. This state is normally experienced for a brief moment when time dilation occurs, and often great insights and wisdom are glimpsed. Some artists have been able to draw while they are asleep, yet upon waking up they do not have the ability to draw. These phenomena cannot be explained, but with modern technology, we can capture it on film and brain scans and observe this. Practicing *nidra* yoga, the yoga of total relaxation, you can cultivate the ability to extend the *turia* time, where your brain is emitting the delta waves.

When this cave of brahma is awakened and stimulated, it can feel like a geyser or a fountain. You could visualize it like the fountain that comes out from the blowhole of a whale, coming up and out from your crown. You could have a sense of ejaculating inside your head in the cave of brahma, which can feel like fireworks going off.

Tantric Secret

If the sexual arousal is too much to sustain, you can manage the energy, directing it upwards. Imagine it coming out of the top of your crown and then cascading down over the body. Stroke the energy up on the body from the genitals to the crown and down again. You can also focus on the micro-cosmic orbit and the infinity shape around your body, as well as putting your tongue up to the roof of the mouth to direct the energy. This may result in a most incredible experience that could stay with you for a long while. This knowledge is part of an initiation into tantric practices that direct potent energy and distribute it.

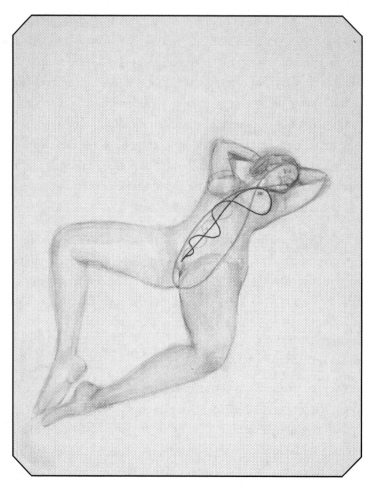

Image 38: Female Figure Front

Testimonial

I feel the type of peace I get from a meditation sitting, but I also feel connected with my sexual chakra and a deep sense of satisfaction. (S.K.)

Taking the raw sexual energy, and directing it up through the cave of brahma will create more powerful orgasms that just keep coming and washing through your whole being.

CHAPTER 20:

Your Largest Sexual Organ

T HERE IS ANOTHER SEX secret, most effective in male sexual performance and health. Your largest and most important sexual organ is not the brain, nor your genitals, nor is it the eyes or skin, nor the nose or tongue, though all these help your sexual arousal and sexual satisfaction. It is actually your arteries and the blood vessels, more specifically, the inner lining in the blood vessels. The epithelium is the inner lining in your arteries that produces a chemical called nitric oxide.

Nitric oxide relaxes the muscles and increases the blood flow everywhere in your body. Your genitals work as hydraulics: the more blood flows to the genitals, the stronger the erections. Conjure up the analogy with the image of a fireman's hydraulic hosepipe on a reel. When there is no water pressure, the pipe is soft, and when the water pressure is turned on, water pressure is high and the pipe is erect.

L-Arginine supplements can help increase nitric oxide in the body.

Be aware that medications to reduce blood pressure will have an effect on your sexual performance. So can medications for heart conditions and diabetes. Be very cautious about Viagra and similar substances. They may help with temporary erection, but they also are extremely dangerous to your heart. Some cancer treatments and medications will have an impact on the libido and effect sexual performance, as well as the oestrogens and testosterone levels.

Make sure you research diligently and consult your doctors. Seek second opinions from reputable practitioners. Be aware that some doctors over-prescribe medications either as a caution or due to the fact that they are sponsored by a pharmaceutical company. The good news is there are ways to heal this, with the correct food, supplements, herbs, and mind-training.

Tantric practices also teach about new ways of making love. Tantric practices, such as the karezza meditations, can bring much pleasure to both partners even if erection is not a possibility. The energetic connection is more important. The emphasis for a mechanical connection in a friction-based idea of sexual performance drops. Instead, the electro-magnetic connection between the love partners' genitals is more important.

After a practice of approximately forty-two minutes of a 'non-doing' sexual meditation, a shift in the energy can occur naturally. This could result in deeply profound orgasms that are not based in friction sex, and they can even occur within the woman when her male partner is flaccid. This may sound far-fetched, but it is an old tantric practice.

After travels in the East, Alice Bunker Stockham, the first female doctor in America, taught a technique called karezza, a form of relaxed genital connection which led to a very different experience of sex and orgasm. Modern neuroscience has begun to understand this as a way of avoiding the dopamine dip after conventional orgasm which leads to disharmony.

Chapter 21:

Penis, Lingam, Vajra

THE PENIS IN TIBETAN is called vajra, meaning 'diamond', 'hardness', or 'thunderbolt lightening'. 'Lingam' is the Hindi word meaning 'the magic wand of light'. Healing occurs on all levels of your being when honouring the vajra.

You can experience high sexual arousal and ejaculation control by practicing the breathing PC muscles and relaxation techniques as described earlier.

When you are experiencing prolonged and heightened erotic arousal, this will result in increased dopamine levels. In a man it produces the experience of the 'happy, feel-good' euphoric neurotransmitters. As mentioned before, increased levels of dopamine will aid in alleviating symptoms of Parkinson's disease. The aim is to enable Shiva, the man god, to experience more energy and relaxation. When the vajra is soft, be gentle; when it is erect, use firmer touch. Move energy around, alternate between different strokes, and spread the energy around the body, down the legs and up the arms, inscribing the figure eight on his body.

Agree before starting the massage that he will inform you when he has reached number eight. As previously described, number eight is the orgasmic peak. As he relaxes, the orgasmic peak will become the orgasmic plateau. Zero is sleep state, totally relaxed. Nine is down the slope, beginning to ejaculate. Ten is one-hundred-per-cent ejaculated, totally spent. To spread the energy when Shiva is highly aroused, put one thumb on the medulla oblongata and one on the third eye. Shiva can focus on the space between and breathe in while pulling the energy up his body and releasing it. Direct Shiva to put his tongue to the roof of the mouth.

Allow the orgasmic waves, riding the waves of orgasmic bliss without ejaculating, to repeat several times. At the fourth time it will reach the heart chakra. After at least three cycles or waves, the need to ejaculate will dissipate naturally. Shiva could experience a level of satiation he has never known before. Alternatively you can use the 'big draw' technique. Shiva tenses everything in his body and pulls everything and all energy inwards and holds it. When he can no longer hold it, he exhales audibly and releases. This will usually leave Shiva in a very sensitive condition. It is best to wrap him up in the towels or a blanket and just sit with him for a while without touching him, so he can experience the ripples of energy.

When massaging and honouring the vajra, make sure you use plenty of lubricant. Always remember while honouring that there is a god on the other end of the vajra! Look at him, and witness his pleasure and bliss. This gesture of looking without judgment in itself could be a huge transformation and healing for him – to be witnessed in his passion, his power, and his vulnerability.

Testimonial

I can still feel some lovely sensual energies flowing through my body. It's like you're there giving me permission to open up to these energies, let them flow and enjoy them. I feel so close to you at those times. (A.V.)

MALE PERFORMANCE: ERECT VS. FLACCID

Erection is synonymous with expectation, from both male and female. It is a commonly mistaken idea that an erection must be maintained in order to be aroused. It is not common knowledge that a flaccid vajra/ lingam/penis, is actually more sensitive. When a man becomes sexually aroused, the brain sends the signals and the chemical, nitric oxide, is excreted in the blood vessels' inner linings that helps relaxation and so allows more blood to flood into the penis, resulting in an erect penis.

For both men and women, when you are sexually aroused the genitals are engorged with blood. The brain also excretes a unique cocktail of opiates – chemicals such as endorphins, dopamine, cortisol, and melatonin, which is a hormone produced in the pineal gland which affects the libido, sexual appetite and at night it regulates sleep/wake cycles and is a natural anti-oxidant playing an important part in the ageing process, cancer treatment and much more. These can have an anaesthetic effect. The pain threshold rises during arousal. This means that during arousal, a person can sustain more intensity, even higher levels of pain, than when they are not sexually aroused. Therefore, when the penis is erect, it is in fact less sensitive and can take more direct stimulation. It is a paradox that when the vajra is flaccid, it is more sensitive, and as you stimulate the vajra and it becomes aroused, it will be less sensitive.

Barry Long was a tantric master from Australia; he suggested that the vajra is only meant to be erect when inside the yoni. He explained that if the vajra is erect anywhere outside the yoni, then the person is not living in the moment but in the future, anticipating the sexual act. I concur with some of his teachings, though I believe an aroused man can have an erection, as this is a natural part of the experience and pleasures. The key is to relax and enjoy a great erection. At the same time, be aware that a man could have and give great pleasure and orgasms even when the vajra is flaccid. (See the karezza sexual mediation.) Either way, allow yourself to enjoy the experience. I would like to commend you for reading this far. Please send an email info@tantra.uk.com, quoting THBG, to receive your special bonus gift.

Having an erection does not mean that either of you needs or has to do anything about it. It is a completely natural process. The issue is what responsible, empowered, and appropriate action will be taken or not taken. An erection is entirely the responsibility of the man. There is no need to act upon it, and certainly there is no need for it to result in sexual intercourse or ejaculation. Holding space for your lover, Shiva, could take him beyond the perceived experience into a new realm, facilitating a new experience for Shiva. These experiences are shared here throughout the book through testimonials. This can only occur when sexual energy is harnessed and transmuted, transformed into the fuel for enlightenment or bliss, as a state of being.

Testimonial

'I do feel that I am arriving home – the place I have dreamed of – I now know where to find it … beyond the beyond … ' (D.B.)

CHAPTER 22:

Tantric Lovers Rituals

RITUALS ARE CENTRAL TO tantra and are a tantric practice, a *sadhana*. A tantric practitioner needs to have their own individual daily practices that sustain and form the basis and foundation of their tantric journey.

The second volume will guide you both in the process. It includes step-by-step guidance on how to implement tantric knowledge into practice and how to create the fertile ground for the tantric magic to arise.

For lovers this can be profound and playful at the same time. Spirituality does not mean you have to be solemn or overly serious. The Dalai Lama is a very happy convivial divine human being. The laughing Buddha is also a beautiful image that can inspire and guide our approach.

Become the process. Just like when you taste a pineapple with all your awareness, you can become the tasting process itself. Where there is no separation between the person tasting and the taste, the same with giving and receiving, all becomes one.

The great secret is to know which parts of the preliminary preparations to use and which to omit. Without the vital awakening of the pathways, the profound results will not arise, just like following a cake recipe. The inner secrets will be revealed when you practice these teachings diligently. You will then gain body/spirit integration and a knowing, from a place of embodying the teachings. The greatly sought 'Ahh!' is in being the process, embodying the teachings. If you choose to, you can enjoy the phenomenal benefits.

PREPARING FOR TANTRIC RITUALS

PRACTICALITIES

All instructions here apply to all genders. We normally think there are only two, though in Thailand and other places in the world there are more categories that are very important to acknowledge and honour. Nowadays with sexual liberation, there are more and more people fitting into the 'meta' and moving away from the 'traditional' ideas. As each individual is unique and creates his or her own sexuality, there could be billions of definitions, so I normally refer to people who do not fit into the stereotypical male/female categories, as the 'meta'. 'Meta' means 'above'.

If you are left-handed or if you wish to change from the suggestions, as long as you are still honouring the sacred and basic fundamental principles as outlined previously, please adapt the instructions to suit your needs.

In tantra yoga we all have the masculine and feminine aspects of our own being. In a gay couple, this is more balanced, as each partner holds both genders. When you are holding space and giving to Shiva, the man, god, you will be assuming the Shakti role. When you are holding space for Shakti, the goddess, woman, and you are her lover, regardless of what gender you are, to balance her energies she will need you to embody the polarity, so you will embody Shiva consciousness and qualities, such as holding space, presence, and awareness.

As the spark of love happens between the lovers, it is similar to the polarities of a battery. Since it is recognized in tantra yoga that all humans contain both aspects, they could embody either at choice. The instructions are directed at you, the giver, whatever gender you embody and regardless of sexual orientation.

The rituals in this book are intended for love partners. The rituals are suitable for gay, bi, and heterosexual couples.

EMBODYING PHYSICAL COMFORT AND EASE

It is very important that you look after yourself when massaging. Keep moving, flowing, and swaying, as if you are dancing. The spine and arms move like an exotic dancer or an artist. Make sure your body is loose, natural, and empty, like a blade of grass in the wind. Avoid tensing up, and remember to breathe out. Exhalation is the key to letting go. This will help eliminate any tension and enable you to be free from pain or discomfort. If you feel physically uncomfortable, make sure you adjust your position. If you feel emotionally awkward, welcome this: it means you are learning something new. As you are observing this, you grow and evolve, flexing your emotional, psychological, and spiritual muscles. By stretching beyond our comfort zone, we evolve spiritually and develop.

Embody the witness consciousness. This is where you observe with interest and curiosity all that arises, without being drawn into the drama or holding judgments if you have been drawn in. Release your identification with your personality, letting go of the ego, of how you are perceived, and of all these exhausting games.

You can just be, in the pure flow of awareness, and become a clear channel for divine energy to flow through you. When you embody the god or the goddess, then you can be in this state, where all knowledge comes to you naturally and effortlessly, arising from pure awareness.

When you are loose, natural, and empty, you become a clear channel to existence itself. Allow the celestial energies such as reiki and other forms of energy to be channelled through you. It can be experienced as if it is not you who is doing the massage, as if you lost your sense of 'self' and became the massage itself. It is not comprehendible with the cognitive mind, but it is a visceral, felt experience. This occurs when you are the conduit, embodying universal energy. It occurs naturally, without you having to do anything.

CENTRING AND GROUNDING

The giver will need to be centred and grounded. Centring and grounding are the terms used for being at ease. They include clarity of presence, solidity, holding and embodying great internal connection to reality and to earth, and being able to function in the world. When some people are excited, they seem to be flying. The image often used is that they appear to be taking off like balloons. Some people are energetically heavy, and they seem to be stuck or unable to move and grow.

Being centred has a sense of ease and grace. You are able to flow with and respond to whatever is occurring, but you will not be blown away should an emotional expression occur in the middle of a session. There is a solid central core to your being. The spine and the central channel, called the *shushumna* in yoga, are depicted as a hollow bamboo, strong and clear to allow energy to flow. Centring yourself is the first step.

SEVEN QUALITIES OF PRESENCE

Make sure you are totally present for the receiver. The seven qualities necessary to being present are:

1. clarity

2. kindness

3. unconditional love

4. compassion

5. curiosity, being interested in seeing what will unfold

6. non-judgmental witnessing

7. generosity of being

These qualities will enable the receiver to experience safety and will allow them to relax and let go, to surrender into your trusted hands.

As you enter into an altered state of consciousness while you are massaging, the swaying, dancing, and flowing around their body will help ground you.

RHYTHM

Maintaining a consistent rhythm throughout the tantric healing massage is important. Keep the rhythm slow and constant. The receiver will be able to relax into an altered state of consciousness.

Chanting, singing mantras and sacred words, will honour the beloved, as previously described. This will also help you to use the BSM keys: breath, sound, and movement.

Breath, sound, and movement will help the dance of Shakti energy, transforming the ordinary human being into to a divine incarnation of the god or goddess.

SMELL

Due to the intimate nature of the massage, both the giver and receiver need to ensure they are bathed, their teeth are brushed, and their breath is fresh. A bathing ritual could be part of the preamble to the tantric healing massage for lovers and can be an act of honouring and worshipping, connecting on such deep and profound levels.

When the receiver is in a relaxed state and has his eyes closed, at certain times during the honouring rituals the sense of smell will become heightened. The sense of smell is directly connected with the base chakra, our first chakra located at the perineum. Sexual energy is awakened by smell, and at the same time the sense of smell is amplified by the awakened sexual energy.

It will be advisable to avoid eating raw onion and garlic at least one day in advance. The smell of garlic comes through the pores of our skin, and it is more pungent the day after. This could be experienced as repulsive if the partner has not shared the same meal. Smoked fish, sea food, and spicy food could have a similar affect, so be mindful; 'what you eat is what you are.' Coconut, pineapple, and mango fruit and drinks do wonders for the smell, the taste of semen, and intimacy.

Due to the nature of the tantric healing massage, the senses will be heightened and everything will be amplified. Often people report that their sense of smell is stronger during and after a session.

SAFETY

It is advisable to remove all the receiver's jewellery and piercings and certainly to remove jewellery on the hands and neck of the giver, as you will be using these parts of your body to massage.

BOUNDARIES

Be aware when you are massaging a client. Find out if there are any allergies, medical history, current health issues, or emotional states prior to commencing. Make sure you establish boundaries and speak honestly about expectations and agreements. If a client communicates the desire to have sexual intimacy, which is not appropriate, ensure you acknowledge verbally his desire and validate his right to have this desire. Refrain from ridiculing his desires, as he has just taken the risk to expose himself emotionally and he is vulnerable. Make sure you are clear about your boundaries and your agreed course of action.

Prior to commencing, negotiate and establish boundaries that will be respected and adhered to. This is important to ascertain, especially when you are massaging your love partner. In love relationships people sometimes expect their partner to be gifted and to able to read their mind. Some partners take each other for granted in long-term relationships. You may be surprised at the new discoveries that will be like gemstones when you take the time to ask what your partner needs, his or her wishes and aspirations.

Listen attentively to what your partner says, as if they are the most interesting lover you are with for the very first time, which at this moment they are. Treat your long-term lover as if they matter. Show that you have so much love and time for them. This simple action of really listening with interest will transform and enhance your relationship. This will enable your beloved to feel safe and know that the boundaries will be respected and that their emotional wellbeing will be honoured. Boundaries will help the receiver to feel safe and held, enabling them to relax completely.

MUSIC

Music in the background is important to help create an atmosphere or erotic spiritual ambiance. The most important music is the internal music that you will be sharing with your beloved, as the massage is like playing a rare instrument of the divine. Honour the beloved by chanting while you are massaging him or her.

There are many devotional music CDs. In my opinion the best is by Craig Pruess, the album series of *Sacred Chants for Tantric Lovers*, *Sacred Chants of Devi*, *Sacred Chants of Shiva*, and *Sacred Chants of Buddha*. The DVD set and the CDs are available through Transcendence Tantra (www.tantra.uk.com). These chants and sounds have energetic resonance that permeates into the core of your being, as well as creating a sacred atmosphere and clearing any negative energy that may be a residue from previous encounters.

Choose background music that will transport the receiver and the giver into being the tantric divine couple, where time stands still and you bask in erotic sensuality. Other than sacred Sanskrit devotional chants and mantras, music without words in a comprehensible language is best, as the mind will not be able to hold on to the words.

It is best to use only one song or chant for the whole massage, so as to enable you both, the receiver and the giver, to go into an altered state of consciousness. Maybe you wish to choose different chants of music for each ritual. Choosing the mantra is so important, as you will absorb energetically the essence of the chant and the mantra. It will have physical repercussions on your wellbeing.

Chapter 23:

The Physical Environment

Creating Sacred Ritual Space

A CONDUCIVE ENVIRONMENT IS PARAMOUNT to a tantric healing massage. Tantra is about spaciousness. If the massage is to be done in a cluttered space, you can drape beautiful materials to cover the clutter. Luxurious imagery will help conjure up the feeling of spaciousness and abundance.

It is preferable to be in a warm, spiritually conducive place to practice. You can create such an environment by using a dedication ceremony, intentions, and a space-clearing ritual, or even simply by spreading a different bed cover on the area which will be dedicated for the tantric healing massage. This could be a large duvet on the floor.

Image 39: Temple Environment

Use appropriate devotional artwork and music, erotic tantric images, flowers, and spiritual artefacts such as stones, crystals, statues, and peacock feathers – anything that is meaningful to you and your beloved.

Make sure all phones are switched off while you are practicing together. In fact, it would be beneficial to have these items removed from the space all together. If you have young children, make sure you have a plan in place for their safe care so you will not be distracted.

Give yourselves plenty of time. Tantra is about spaciousness. Two hours is the minimum to set aside for a massage. If you are going through all the rituals shared here, you will need about twenty hours!

Prepare, discuss, design, and create this space, choosing together the artefacts and the layout. Working together on this joint venture will mean you are both contributing your energies to the creation of the tantric space, and it will feel owned by both of you.

Having a specially designed temple or a dedicated room for tantric ritual practice is wonderful, but for most people you can simply mark a space as sacred by creating intentions, dancing, singing, and doing the invocation ritual. You can obtain a copy of the Invocation Ritual and the 12 Tantric Directions Booklet through www.tantra.uk.co or email info@tantra.uk.com.

Space clearing can be done by sounding gongs, symbols, horns, clapping, and sounding *Aum* or by playing tantric music such as *Tantra Dorje Ling* by David Parson, or Craig Pruess's *Sacred Chants of Devi* or *Sacred Chants of Shiva*.

ERGONOMICS AND MASSAGE SURFACE

Using a comfortable foam mattress or memory foam on the floor will allow the masseur to have easy access all over the body without having to break the flow of the sequence. A spring mattress would be disruptive as you move around the receiver. This could disrupt the deep and tranquil state they may have contacted.

A massage table could also be used, though it would be preferable to work on the floor or a large futon bed where the masseur will be on the same level as the receiver. This ensures that you, as the giver, are part of the process and are not removed clinically from the receiver. A feeling of separation can arise through using a table and also through wearing a white coat as some massage therapists sometimes use. Energetically it can feel like a barrier, a form of protection, preventing merger with the other. It could create a feeling of abandonment or even bring up issues of inequality.

When massaging on a foam mattress on the floor, you can use your body weight to apply more pressure if needed. You may prefer to use a table if you experience back problems. However, through movement and modifications to your posture, you may find that you are able to work on the floor.

Case Study

A student (A.S.) at a tantric massage weekend workshop insisted on working on a massage table. He reported that due to his long-term back pain the 'long full-length body strokes with both hands are just too difficult for me, with my back. The weekend was a very powerful experience. It was amazing sharing it with my partner. The final sequence from her was unforgettable. But when it was my turn to give, I struggled throughout the weekend with the weakness in my back due to scoliosis. The table did not really help.' I suggested a modification, introducing swaying and working on the floor. He responded, 'I have given two sessions this week, and they both worked really well.'

You could make or purchase a special cover to go over your mattress, futon, or massage table, a cover that will signify that something special and extraordinary is taking place. An area of at least three metres (three yards) by two metres (two yards) is best. The receiver lies in the middle, and you have equal space around them for your working platform. As the sequence works around the whole of the body, every part is given equal attention.

The person giving the massage using a table may find that they are straining to reach the other side, and this could be more damaging to the practitioner.

You will need an assortment of cushions or pillows of various sizes to hand. These are useful for propping up the recipient's knees, and they also provide a comfortable place for the masseur to work from. Place cushions under the arch of the foot and the shin of the leg if needed when the receiver is lying on their front, and possibly under the belly or the chest as well. It is best to have their head as straight and in as natural a line with the spine as possible.

You will need clean sheets and towels to lie on and also to keep the person receiving feeling safe, clean, and warm. Dark colour towels are best. The red colour feels more luxuriant. White or cream colours could feel rather clinical. Velvet material will absorb oil without showing stains. The sheets and towels are for the receiver to lie upon and possibly at the end of the massage, if needed, they can be wrapped with the towels as if in a cocoon.

A comfortably heated room will be more conducive to the massage and the comfort of the receiver. Additional heaters may be required and it is best that they be readily available nearby in case the receiver feels cold suddenly.

A sudden change in the receiver's feeling of temperature can indicate a shift in their emotional release or an energetic state. A thermometer will provide an objective indication of the actual temperature once you have warmed the environment to their desired level of comfort. Have additional heaters or an air conditioner unit that you can easily control and adjust, which will result in rapid change of temperature.

The ideal temperature is very individual. Some people prefer it very hot and others less so. Therefore a heated under-blanket will help create a warm nest for the receiver to lie on. The best are the under-blankets you can easily adjust with various temperature settings. Make sure you remember to switch it on prior to the massage starting and off afterwards.

Having a checklist is helpful. It may seem obvious, but with a checklist you can just relax, knowing you have covered all preparations and can be totally present with your partner.

Since you as the giver will be moving around and will be physically dynamic and active, you may become very hot. Keeping the receiver warm while you, the giver, are cooler would be advantageous.

A menopausal woman giving a tantric massage will need to manage the environment in an innovative way, as she can keep herself cool with a fan pointing at her upper body, while an electric blanket will provide extra heat for her partner receiving. Additional heaters pointing at the feet and or the top of the head will help keep the receiver warm.

When massaging the back during kundalini activation, it is best to keep the receiver's head straight in line with the spine, maintaining a natural curve of the spine as possible. You could use a U-shaped neck pillow or alternatively a rolled up towel curved as a U to support the forehead. Make sure your partner can breathe easily if they are lying on a foam mattress on the floor rather than on a table with a headrest attachment or a special hole cut out.

The table head attachment and the hole cut out in the table are not as good as they may seem for this kind of tantric healing massage, as the spine and head are not following the natural curve, but rather emphasizing the top of the neck.

A foam surface or a duvet on the floor is best. It is cheaper, and it allows you to create a tantric space anywhere, as well as being able to move around the body and be part of the process. Ergonomically and physically working on a surface on the floor is far superior to a purpose-built table which will be too small and not conducive for this type of massage.

HYGIENE

It is important to have healthy hands. Keep the nails short and smooth. Ensure there are no open cuts on your hands. Have access to warm water and hand sanitizer, soap, and a towel to make sure your hands are kept clean prior to the massage and after.

You will need nitrile, non-latex, or similar surgical gloves. Normally one session could consume at least three gloves when giving a prostate massage, two from the back and one from the front. You will need spare gloves available as they may tear, thus ensuring the flow of the massage in uninterrupted.

Nitrile gloves are the best to use It is highly advisable to use gloves when you are facilitating an internal yoni, vulva, or anal massage for a client other than your lover. Always ensure you are using gloves for protection from STIs. Nitrile gloves are non-allergenic, non-latex gloves, and the gloves will not degrade when using oils.

SEXUALLY TRANSMITTED INFECTIONS

As a practitioner, you have an ethical responsibility to be aware of and be able to identify signs of sexually transmitted infections (STIs). Familiarize yourself with the latest research. It is freely available on the internet. You will also find information from government institutions, clinics, hospitals, and universities.

Some people are not aware of the implications of STIs and some don't even know what state of health they are in. Some people may carry chlamydia unknowingly, which can affect their fertility and their ability to conceive.

Some individuals may be carriers of a form of herpes that may not show externally. This could have a serious effect on others, even though it may not affect the carrier. Herpes spores could still be shed (drop off) and transmitted, even when there is no visible sign of the condition. Herpes,

HIV, and AIDS are all viruses that can be passed on during sex, but they cause different symptoms and health problems.

Some STIs are viral, while others are bacterial. Some will live a short period of time and are easily destroyed by proper use of soap and sanitizers. Others will be more robust and hardy and are not affected by ordinary hygiene products. Hydrogen peroxide is used in some tantra schools to wash genitals and mouth after sexual contact, as it releases oxygen which is a natural disinfectant.

HPV, the genital human papillomavirus virus, is the most common sexually transmitted infection. There are more than forty strains of HPV that infect the genitals, mouth, and throat. 90 per cent of cases clear within two years naturally. Some HPV will persist and will manifest as genital warts, rarely as cases of throat warts, RRP (recurrent respiratory papillomatosis, which in children is called JORRP), and cervical cancers of the vulva, vagina, penis, anus, and oropharynx, which is the back of throat including the base of tongue and the tonsils. The Cervarix and Gardasil vaccines are used by the medical profession to provide protection from HPV that cause most cervical cancers and genital warts.

There are many places for STI information and many places you can get yourself tested. Some practitioners will treat all clients as if they are carriers of all conditions. Thus their practice is healthy to both client and practitioner.

Some people may have more than one lover. When one is having unprotected sexual intimacy with more then one lover, in regards to STIs, the risk factor the medical model employs, it is as if they are having sexual intercourse with 600 people. .

Thinking positive thoughts is great, but it does not protect you from STIs. Being an adult means being able to discuss sexuality and any STIs you may have had prior to having sexual intimacy with a new lover. It is best to deal with reality responsibly, as people may have different types of relationship and intimacy agreements.

CHAPTER 24:

Models of Relationships

I T IS COMMENDABLE TO have the ability to engage in intimate relationships and thrive. The blessings are profound and beyond measure. There are a few models of relationship that are common around the world, including monogamy, polygamy, polyandry, polyamory, open relationships, and affairs. As tantra embraces and welcomes all aspects of our being, it is important to openly acknowledge the various models of relationships. There are other forms of relationships, though the main six are the most common. When working with a client, never judge their beliefs or way of life. Unconditional regard and acceptance is vital in this world.

Monogamy is the practice of having one committed relationship or partnership. This is the most common relationship in Western civilization and in Judaic and Christian cultures.

Polygamy is the practice in some cultures of a man having committed relationships with more than one female partner, such as in some Islamic societies or some of the Mormon societies.

Polyandry is the practice of one woman having committed relationships with more than one male partner. It may be due to the fact that traditionally there is no war in these regions and parts of the culture, and therefore there are more men to share. It is natural in some parts of the Canadian Arctic, American indigenous people, the first inhabitants of the Canary Islands, some Polynesian societies, Tibet, Bhutan, Nepal,

Sri Lanka, China, Nigeria, and the Maasai society in the Saharan Africa, Kenya, and Tanzania.

Polyamory is the practice of having committed relationships with more than one partner. The emphasis here is on ethical behaviour and commitment. It is common nowadays for people to want to have multiple partners and to normalize this as a social acceptance. There are many people nowadays identifying themselves as polyamorous, without engaging in conscious relating, and thus the term has taken on another meaning altogether – polyf**kery. The definition of polyamory is used all too readily without the commitment part. Polyamory takes a lot of time in managing emotions in the complex web of many levels of relationships. The key here is conscious relating.

In **open relationships** the love partners are aware and consent to engaging with intimate relationships, with the partners choosing to have their own individual experience outside the marriage or commitment. For this model to be successful and mutually satisfactory, both partners need to feel secure and confident within themselves and their relationship, which requires commitment and agreements.

In the case of **affairs**, the love partners are engaging in intimate relationships with other partners while choosing to keep the affair secret and hidden from the other partner. For the most part, this is deceitful and can evoke many patterns from childhood and the re-enactment of some drama. There can also be the thrill of the forbidden, which can be enticing. There are some cases where the affairs could be necessary for the wellbeing of the couple, for example, in cases of one partner's chronic health condition. The ethics vary from cultures and the individual's experiences.

CHAPTER 25:

Space Preparation

Image 40: Creating a Temple Environment

S ET THE SCENE THOUGHTFULLY. You will need to prepare in advance the space, the time, and the props to help you, including music, flowers, etc. Spontaneity takes a lot of planning!

Flowers are for honouring. Flower petals are wonderful to have sprinkled on the body, and lying in a bed of flower petals is an honouring experience and feels luxuriant. Most of us may experience this on our wedding day or anniversary. Imagine how wonderful it will be to step onto a tantric environment where you are walking on flower petals.

Helping the receiver remember and accept their divine nature is profoundly honouring. Prepare the environment thoughtfully.

Make sure you have to hand feathers, silk, chiffon, fur, different textures that will feel sensual and erotic when stroked on the skin.

Prepare in advance an assortment of fruit, beverages, and aphrodisiac food, such as sensual deserts to use as an honouring of the beloved in the Awakening the Senses ritual. For erotic cookery ideas, see the *Naked Tantric Chef* cookery book, available through www.tantra.uk.com. There are also sample recipes in the appendix.

Have to hand tissues, in case of an emotional release.

EMPTY BLADDER

Make sure both you and the receiver have an empty bladder before the session begins. Then you will know that when the female partner who is receiving feels the urge to urinate during the massage, it is more likely that she is experiencing female ejaculation. This will also help avoid any disruption to the flow of the session by either of you needing to leave to use the bathroom.

As mentioned before, in yoga the *ojas*, the life-force energy juices, are present in the female and male ejaculation. These are highly potent and nourishing; they are the elixir of life and youth.

Have at hand plenty of towels to allow the woman to feel safe, to be able to let go, and to allow herself the possibility of experiencing female ejaculation.

MASSAGE OILS

You will need plenty of high-quality unscented sweet almond oil, rape-seed oil, or coconut oil. Castor oil is best to help heal scar tissue. Ensure you are aware of any nut allergies in the case of using almond oil. One complete massage could use a lot of oil. This, of course, will vary greatly according to the different body size and skin absorption. Alternatively, you can use talcum powder if the receiver dislikes oil.

Sweet almond or coconut oil is the best. Coconut oil, also known as coconut butter, will need to be melted, as it is solid at moderate room temperature. Warm oils create an immediate effect of receptivity and a sense of allowing and relaxation. It feels wonderful having warm oil touch on the body. You could also use cheaper oils such as rapeseed oil; they are just as good. The intention is to have a smooth flow of touch, ensuring the drag and pull on the skin is reduced.

Also be mindful to avoid any breakouts and inflamed areas or sensitive skin. For internal yoni/vulva massage, water-based lubricants would be best. Natural raw coconut oil, which is not water-based, is also regarded as one of the best mediums. Coconut oil is used as an aphrodisiac. Coconut oil has an arousing scent, feels sensual, and gives a natural arousing sensation. It has a viscosity similar to natural yoni lubrication.

Choose essential oils that would be suitable for direct contact with the skin. Always ensure you are aware of any allergies prior to the rituals starting. Make sure you know the correct amount to use for diluting with water or oil.

If using scented oils, make sure the receiver is not allergic to the ingredients. Do take care to avoid using scented oils internally and on the genitals. Artificial oils may cause irritation or aggravate dormant skin conditions.

Always apply oil to your own hand. Avoid applying directly onto the body. If the oil is too hot, it can cool in the palm of your hand. If the oil is too cold, it will warm in the palm of your hand. The sensation of a loving hand spreading the oil can be phenomenal. Drizzling oil directly on the body may sometimes feel clinically removed and jarring for the receiver. The intention is to make the receiver feel connected, grounded, and blissful.

ENERGY FLOW

Be aware of the direction and the flow of energy. The body is the container for the energy to flow within. The life-force energy is existence itself flowing through you. Be very cautious when others tell you that you are 'blocked' at a certain chakra, as the energy in chakras changes throughout the day according to experience and feelings. When a person hears some 'authority' pronouncing they have a 'blockage' at a certain place, their mind will tend to play the words over and over, making it a self-fulfilling prophecy.

When you are facilitating a massage or working as a talking therapist, be aware when you are receiving or 'picking up' the energy that is given off by the other person. This is termed 'transference'. When you are responding to or acting out something that is clearly from the other, this is known as 'projected identification'. There are instances in some clients' sessions where you may have been feeling totally alert, but in their presence you suddenly feel unusually tired. In situations where you have established empathy or merged and identified with them in some way, you could also 'pick up' and act out on their emotions, such as anger, especially when they are unable to connect to it themselves.

Be vigilant when some unusual feeling arises while you are massaging. It could be an indication of some energetic shift or an emotional release occurring and you are picking it up. Make a mental note on how you are feeling prior to the session commencing. Being able to deal with this will require proper training and personal experience. Supervision by a qualified and experienced practitioner, who also trained in psychotherapy, will provide support, insights, and guidance. You are creating the container which is the holding space and creating safety for your lover to be able to just let go into bliss, healing, or expanded pleasure.

CHAPTER 26:

Two Rituals

WHO IS IT FOR?

It is suitable for everyone, including all sexual orientations.

To emphasis again, the rituals in this book are intended for love partners. The rituals are suitable for gay, bi, and heterosexual couples. The instructions are directed at you, the giver, whatever gender you embody. The instructions for the receiver will need to be appropriate if you are working with a man or a woman, regardless of sexual orientation.

HONOURING RITUAL – FOOT MASSAGE

This ritual can be done on its own or as a preparation for the tantric healing massage.

Let the beloved be seated on a chair and kneel by their feet. Honour your beloved with a foot washing and massage ritual prior to commencing. This is to be done reverently and lovingly.

Place the foot of your beloved onto your heart chakra. This can be done before, during, or after the foot massage, while you are looking into the eyes of your lover, the divine god or goddess. Use warm water to cleanse their feet. You can apply warm oil to anoint each foot. Remember, less is more. Do not concern yourself with reflexology techniques. More important is holding the foot of the divine on your heart chakra or in your hands and looking at them with reverence. Be mindful, this is not a master-slave scenario but a highly revered position, as you are the divine's consort. This honouring could take between fifteen minutes up to an hour.

BATHING RITUAL

Having the bathing ritual as part of preparation for the tantric healing massage, or as a ritual on its own, will be wonderful for the receiver. It is a preamble to the tantric healing massage. This reminds the receiver of the luxurious nature of the massage. It helps in accepting the divine nature of your humanity, and it is profoundly honouring.

You can have a bathtub prepared with flower petals and essential oils. Sitting by the side or behind your beloved, you can honour them and wash their body as if you are touching the divine. Ensure the essential oils used have a suitable pleasant aroma and your beloved has no allergies to any of the ingredients.

You can also use a water bowl. Bathe the beloved with warm towels soaked in a portable water bowl, with tea lights underneath to keep the water warm. Make sure you have a special stand for the water bowl, a tray for the tea light candles, and matches or a lighter. Sprinkle rose petals or orchids in the water and choose aromatherapy oils to dilute in the water.

It is a most wonderful experience to be towelled down with warm towels as a way to start the massage, as you can facilitate more relaxation in the body and deepen the experience. Apply the hot towel to the body, starting at the sacrum and wiping down the legs, then up the spine, the back of the heart chakra, across the shoulders, and down the arms.

A full bathing ritual will be done prior to the body imprint ritual, which will be described in this book, as part of the preparation. This honouring could take at least half an hour. Alternatively, you can use hot towels as part of the massage opening sequence. Placing hot towels on the back and apply pressure slowly, towelling and working your way over the whole body. This can offer the feeling of being honoured as a divine and allows the receiver to feel safe and let go.

Prepare a couple of bowls of water filled with hot water and some essential oils, such as a couple of drops of bergamot (check for skin sensitivity) or neroli, jasmine, rose, sandalwood or ylang-ylang. Essential oils can be luxurious and will help open up the chakras and receptivity. Different scents support different intentions. For example, lavender will help relax, bergamot brings the quality of confidence, neroli and ylang-ylang, patchouli and jasmine, induce more erotic receptivity. Explore which scents are pleasant to you and which you are drawn to.

Ensure you wring the hot wet towels thoroughly prior to applying them to the receiver's body. Feather stroke any excess of dampness so the receiver will feel comfortable. Be careful to use the right amount of heat on the body. Also when applying to the eyes, ensure the water is clean, as essential oils will irritate the eyes.

Having rose petals in the water will release natural oils and look beautiful as an offering of honouring.

CONCLUSION:

This Is the Beginning of Your Tantric Journey

THIS BOOK HAS PROVIDED you with the understanding of what is tantra and how tantric lovers can connect sexuality and spirituality, taking their love to a new heights and depths at the same time. We are emotional beings. We all need and yearn for touch in order to thrive. We respond best to kindness, compassion, and love. Touch nourishes the soul; it allows us to flourish. Some clients seek a massage, as they may be in long-term relationships which are devoid of touch and intimacy. Just looking into the eyes with care and a loving touch can transform how we feel and the whole experience of life. Some people wish to discover their sensual selves, the core of their being.

Life is happening right now all around you. This is your time. If you believe in reincarnation, then in the next lifetime you will not be in this body as yourself. If you do not believe in reincarnation, then certainly this is your one chance in this life, in this body, as yourself. Either way, this is it! Wake up and live your life, manifest what you desire, and make a contribution to the people you touch. This is not a dress rehearsal. Live it remembering you are no-thing other than a stage name for the divine!

I wish you a most wonderful journey of discovery and hope that you will experience the *amrita*, a taste of bliss.

I commend you for your courage to embark upon this most phenomenal path of enlightenment that celebrates our sexuality and all aspects of our humanity.

There are some testimonials by people who have been touched by my teachings and practices, who applies themselves and it has changed their lives profoundly, these are attempts to describe the indescribable. Due to the sensitive nature of my work and because sexuality affects every aspect of our lives, people from all over the world like to have me as their best kept secret! It is a privilege and an honour to be able to touch so many people and contribute to their lives and help them enhance their relationships.

Of course, you and I, we are the pioneers changing society and the world as we speak. Practicing tantra and tantric healing massage will propel people to a higher level of consciousness and deeper and more meaningful relationships, discovering new dimensions of our being that seem to have opened up as we have grown in our human spiritual evolution.

As attitudes change and you open to new experiences, you will evolve and will enhance the lives of people that you will touch with your presence, awareness, perhaps even a brief look. Maybe you will be connecting with someone in a brief moment of recognition as you pass by in the street, and an energetic transmission will affect their lives forever! We are beings greater than our own physical bodies, we are also beings of energy, and we are of the light. Ultimately we are all connected, so your happiness will contribute to the well-being of the world.

I would love to hear about your success stories. As mentioned before, sexuality affects every aspect of our being. You may find that these practices will have an unexpected positive repercussion on your professional work and relationships as some of my clients have experienced. In fact, they may affect every aspect of your being.

I wish you all that you desire, and a most enlightening path of self-discovery, healing, the yoga of relationships, and the art of honouring sacred sexuality, that is tantra.

The singer Sting was reported to have said about tantra and his wife: 'Sex is only the surface. Tantra is … about reconnecting with the world of the spirit through everyday things … My church happens to be the person I live with. She is my connection to the sacred.'

It is through others, through relationships, that we thrive, grow, and realize our magnificence and the magnitude of the human power in intention (*bahawana* in Sanskrit, *BeCHavana* in Hebrew) or in actions and the power of words even if they are whispered.

I invite you to live fully your magnificence and enjoy the journey of discovery for your purpose here on our beautiful planet earth. How we are, what we do, and the words we utter make a difference. Even a glance can contribute to the well-being of others.

I look forward to hearing from you about your journey and success stories in life and relationships. Your presence here is a blessing. You are like a fountain overflowing with energy and light. Allow others to drink from the well of your being. Let the drops of your fountain of unconditional love touch the people around you. They will feel the transmission of energy and will be enriched for it.

In this book I have provided you with the necessary background to be able to carry out a tantric honouring of your beloved through tantric practices. In my next book I will be guiding you step by step in the most profound tantric rituals, and my unique tantric healing massage techniques will be presented in the third book. I also share tantric cookery secrets in the *Naked Tantric Chef* book. (See appendix III at the end of this book.)

Thank you for reading this book.

This is the beginning of Your Tantric Journey!

Enjoy and thrive and I would love to hear your success stories.

Wishing you all the love and blessings that you desire.

Hanna, Maha Shakti Kali Ma.

Take a glimpse into the next three books. This will change your life. The skill will enhance your intimacy and elevate it into divine communion. Go ahead and turn the page …

APPENDIX I:

Tantric Rituals for Lovers

(Extracts from the Second Book by Hanna Katz-Jelfs)

The Tantric Invocation Ritual is part of creating the tantric space. This part of the ritual could take from quarter of an hour up to an hour.

SEEING THE BELOVED

Stand opposite your beloved, just looking, making eye contact and tuning in to each other.

Whilst looking at each other, gently sway and move the dance of Shiva and Shakti, the god and the goddess as if you are making love with your eyes, your heart, and your touch.

Image 41: Holding the divine

Caress each other's arms, head, and face.

Tantric Directions Invocation Ritual

Shakti, the goddess, the initiator in tantra, calls in the energies of the wisdom goddesses from all twelve tantric directions (including above, below, and within) and Shiva and Shakti. This part of the ritual can take from half an hour up to an hour. For the complete wording contact www.tantra.uk.com or email nfo@tantra.uk.com.

Here is a sample:

> The eighth direction – North – Air Element, Seeing. In this place we arrive when the cycle is complete. It is the time when we can understand the cycle in a way that is only possible when we live all the stages. Tara is our protective mother as we cross the waters at the end of this cycle. The power of air, wind, and breath, opening our minds to clarity, vision, and understanding. gives wings to our soul and teaches us lightness of being, bringing us intelligence and discernment.

Image 42: Standing *Namaste*

Bring your hands in a prayer gesture in front of your heart, activating your heart chakra with the thumbs touching the centre of your chest. Look at the divine incarnation in your beloved.

Bow your head down slightly. Say, '*Namaste*', meaning 'I salute the divinity within you.' Bring your foreheads together, third eyes touching, while you are still looking into the eyes of the beloved.

After a few minutes which may seem like a timeless eternity, relax and open your hands as a gesture of opening your heart to receive your beloved.

Place your right hand on your beloved's heart chakra at the centre of the chest. Place your own hand on top of theirs. Lean forward and touch your third eyes together while maintaining eye contact.

Stroke each other, enjoying seeing and touching the beloved. Taking your time to savour each caress, as if you are making love to existence itself and you have the whole of eternity, as if time is standing still. Touch as if they are a precious crystal.

ENERGY ANOINTING RITUAL

Stroke the energy from top of the head all the way to the finger tips. Make a gesture of pouring energy onto the crown of your beloved.

Pour energy onto your partner, starting above the crown. Stroke downwards on the body, starting at the crown all the way to the finger tips.

Shakti moves to stand behind Shiva. She could disrobe herself if she chooses. Shakti begins by massaging his head, neck, and shoulders. Continue the stroking down the back, around the buttocks, and up the torso. Press your thumbs into the occipital, towards the medulla oblongata, and then stroke down the spine at the back.

TUNING IN

Sit opposite each other, maintaining a space between knees. Place the left-hand palm facing up, and the right-hand palm facing down. Connect your hands, resting the forearms on the knees and just looking.

Create an infinity knot, with both of your left-hand palms facing upwards and your right-hand palms facing down. Cross your own right-hand wrist over your own left-hand wrist. Connect the palms; this will create a double infinity knot.

Intone and hamonise the universal sound 'Aum' together.

Image 43: Bioresonance

Place your hands on each other's hearts, third eyes touching, looking into the one-eyed god/dess. Allow your heartbeats and the energies from your frontal brain at the third eye connection to be activated and naturally harmonised.

Image 44: *Yab Yum*

Sit in the *yab yum* position. '*Yab yum*' means 'mother/father' in Tibetan. This is the classic tantric position depicted in many tantric sculptures and paintings.

If sitting cross-legged on the floor is not possible, you can sit with your legs open and one partner, traditionally the female, sits on top. You can also try sitting on a chair if you suffer from back problems or flexibility challenges or if you have a different weight ratio with your beloved. Share one breath, as Shiva breathes in, Shakti breathes out, sharing the one breath together.

AWAKENING THE SENSES RITUAL

These are the preliminaries to the tantric healing massage. The body imprint ritual could also be done as a meditation in its own right and would last approximately two hours.

It is important to connect with Shiva's (the god, man) right side first, as it is his masculine side, his cognitive side. Thus he will be more receptive to the energy flow.

Shakti's (the goddess, woman) left side is important to be touched first, as it is her feminine side, her emotional side. Shiva will massage Shakti on her left side first, moving in a clockwise direction up to her head then to her right side and down to her feet.

THE FIVE SENSES

Smell, taste, touch, sound, and sight comprise the basic five senses.

In tantric meditations we transcend above the separation and become one with the object or experience.

As meditations, for example, drop deeper into the experience, taste a pineapple with awareness. You could become the tasting process itself. Where there is no separation between the person tasting and the taste, the same is true with giving and receiving: all become one.

GIVING AND RECEIVING

This can be experienced as one. When you feel both giving and receiving at the same time. This can occur when there are no goals, just the sheer pleasure in being!

Simply enjoy the touch, being held and valued.

The distinction between the giver and the receiver becomes indistinguishable at times. As you drop deeper into meditation, being present unconditionally, you may feel that when you are 'giving' a massage you are feeling energized, as if you are receiving yourself.

TOUCH AS AN ACT OF HONOURING

Honouring is communicated through the touch. Regard and uphold the divine in the beloved. Only in the Awakening the Senses sequence are all types of touch movements to be done upwards on the left side, downwards on the right. The order of these sequences is important, though in neo-tantra the sequences are all mixed together, creating a festival to the senses that is extremely enjoyable and indulgent. The purpose for keeping the sequence in the order described below is to awaken the chakras in order from the base upwards. Smell awakens the base chakra. Taste awakens the second and third chakras. Touch awakens the heart. Sound awakens the throat. Sight awakens the third eye.

Each touch style could be done for a long time, depending on your preference and schedule. If you are only doing Awakening the Senses and Body Imprint, then take your time, savour each action, noticing what your lover's responses are.

The receiver may enjoy one touch, and their body will purr at the touch. They may contract and withdraw at another. Make a mental note. Also, as you repeat this mediation you may notice changes in them; they may begin to love a type of touch that previously they may have been unable to withstand.

Tune in to your beloved. Match your breathing patterns to theirs. If you wish, you can place a blindfold over their eyes, so they can completely let go of pre-empting and anticipation and totally surrender to the experience. being totally there, in the present moment, the gifts it offers and the celebration of hightening the senses.

THE SENSE OF SMELL

Image 45: Smell

Smell is the first and most important sense in the Awakening the Senses honouring ritual. It awakens the first, base chakra, which is connected to our sexuality, sense of survival, and physical well-being.

Use a variety of smells; natural flower scents or essential oils are best. There are also different smells associated with different chakras.

Offer morsels of food and tease the lips. Let him experience the textures, the sensation on the skin, the smells, and the taste. All the different tastes are important to activate.

THE FIVE BASIC TASTES

The five basic tastes are salty, bitter, sweet, sour, and *umami*. *Umami* food comprises flavours such as soy or cheese. Take a sip of drink into your own mouth and transfer the liquid to your beloved's mouth.

BODY IMPRINT RITUAL

This is the name for an honouring ritual of the body, using a variety of touch to awaken, reenergize, and heighten sensitivity. The strokes in body imprint could offer aspects of the six gifts. This is a preparation for the main tantric massage sequence.

THE SIX GIFTS

The six gifts you will be giving as you are being present and touching your beloved will be the following: affirming, honouring, worshipping, healing, teasing, and arousing.

Image 46: Silk

Start with silk, pulling it all over the whole of the body. Shake the material on the receiver's body, and let it glide slowly as it caresses the contours.

Image 47: Touch

Communicate through your touch, the message, 'Here I am, here you are.' Use your fingertips as if you are playing a harp, as light as a feather. Peacock or ostrich feathers feel wonderful on the body. Stroke slowly, using at least two feathers, one in each hand.

Image 48: *Niyasa*

Whisper onto the whole of the body, 'You are my divine god/dess.'

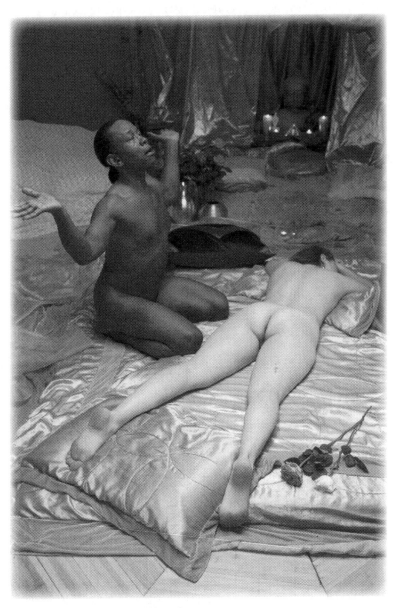

Image 49: *Kum Nye*

Kum nye is a Tibetan healing energy invocation and a yoga practice. Kneel by the side of the beloved, the palms of your hands raised and facing upwards. This gesture collects prana, the life-force energy in the hands.

Have a sense or the intention that energy is streaming through you, as if you are both standing under a divine shower or a celestial waterfall. Receive energy into your crown and hands. Imagine that transparent silver and white droplets are permeating into your being. Feel your heart centre; this is the transformer, converting from Shiva consciousness to pure energy, and from pure raw energy to make more awareness.

Guide your beloved: 'As you breathe in, have a sense of liquid gold percolating through your being, as if you are standing under a divine shower or waterfall.'

For the complete rituals see the second book, *Tantric Rituals for Lovers* by Hanna Katz-Jelfs

APPENDIX II:

Tantric Healing Massage for Lovers

Extracts from the Third Book by Hanna Katz-Jelfs

Use your whole hand to mould around the contours of their body, the tips of the fingers, to the wrists and forearms. Keep the movement fluid, luxuriant, and spacious. It is important to prevent 'snagging'. Place both your hands on the upper back between the shoulder blades, the heel of the hands at the base of the neck. Press down firmly, sliding your hands down the back on either side of the spine.

Image 50: Back Tantric Effleurage

Continue all the way to the lower back and the top of the buttocks. Slide your hands over the side of the buttocks and hips, allowing the whole of your forearm and elbow to be in contact with their back. Glide your hands back up the sides of the torso. Reach the shoulders, continue the 'tantric effleurage' movement by turning your hands, placing your fingers underneath the shoulders. Press down on top of the shoulders.

YONI HONOURING

Image 51: Yoni Honouring

Make sure you are attuned to Shakti. Avoid getting lost in the detail. The key point is to be totally present for your beautiful goddess. Alternate and vary between the different strokes below and stroke energy down legs, round body, arms and head, inscribing the figure of eight. Encourage breathing and movement. Tune in to your beloved goddess.

Image 52: Yoni Connecting

Connecting the yoni and the heart is paramount. Remember this is the yoni-verse of the goddess. Shakti holds within her the secret of life, the universe, existence itself.

For the complete ritual see the third volume, *Tantric Healing Massage Rituals for Lovers* by Hanna Katz-Jelfs. Also the DVDs set *Tantric Healing Massage for Lovers* is available.

Vajra Honouring Ritual

Remind Shiva to indicate when he has reached number eight, the orgasm, prior to ejaculation.

Image 53: Connecting the Vajra and the Third Eye

Stroke the 'spark of light' up the body, from the base chakra all the way up to his third eye and crown. Stroke and spread the energy down the legs. Connecting these parts of the body together. The vajra is the 'tree of life', rooted deep in the body. Always remember while honouring that there is **a god** on the other end of the vajra! Stroke the spark of light up the body, from the base chakra, all the way up to the third eye and the crown at the top of the head. Vibrate both the base chakra and the crown, simultaneously.

DIRECT TRANSMISSION INTO THE HEART

Image 54: The Foot of the Goddess

Place the foot of the god/dess to your heart chakra.

Image 55: Intimacy

Marvel at the beauty of the divine within your partner. Celebrate with gratitude.

For the complete Tantric Healing Massage rituals see the third book, *Tantric Healing Massage Rituals for Lovers* by Hanna Katz-Jelfs. The DVD set *Tantric Healing Massage for Lovers* is also available.

The Naked Tantric Chef Tantric Cookery

Tantric Secrets on How to Improve Your Sex and Spiritual Life through the Food of Love and Tantric Cooking

By The Naked Tantric Chef – Hanna Katz-Jelfs

A glimpse into the Fourth Book

Tasty Sexy Spirituality

Hanna's Divine Bread

¾ cup milk or soy milk

¾ cup water

2 cups plain granary flour. Can use white flour if desired.

2 cups plain whole-meal flour. Can use white flour if desired.

3-5 tablespoons of brown sugar or molasses or honey depending upon desired sweetness.

½ tablespoon salt

1 tablespoon fast-action yeast

3 tablespoons of olive or almond oil

Two handfuls raisins (optional)

Two handfuls pumpkin seeds (optional)

One handful sunflower seeds (optional)

One handful whole nut (optional)

Handful caraway seeds (optional)

Handful of sesame seeds (optional)

Handful of poppy seeds (optional)

1 tablespoon plus cinnamon (optional)

Mix all ingredients and knead until even. Allow for two risings or place in a bread machine. Choose programme setting for French bread or in a preheated oven, set to 160 degree centigrade until desired colour of the crust has been achieved. Length of coking depending on size and depth of tray.

Suggested mantras while preparing: *'Hari Om Tat Sat.'* Alternatively, just say 'love' throughout the preparation.

I SCREAM, ICE CREAM

A very ripe persimmon (also known as sharon fruit). Slice the top as if it will be a hat.

Place in freezer couple of hours before serving just before it freezes hard. This is a natural succulent sorbet.

Sprinkle with desiccated coconut, you can drizzle with Kahlua liquor.

Mantra: *'Hume Hum Braham Hum,'* meaning 'One we are, God we are.'

By Royal Anointment! Cardamom Cream

1 cup double crème

½ cup brown sugar

1 teaspoon grated cardamom

Mix everything in an electric mixer bowl, whisking until stiff

Fresh mint leaves for garnish

Suggested Mantras while preparing: 'My Sweet Lord' (great version by George Harrison

For the complete Top of FormBottom of Form

tantric cookery recipe book, see *The Naked Tantric Chef* by Hanna Katz-Jelfs.

Appendix IV:

Further Reading

Kali's Odiyya: A Shaman's True Story of Initiation by Amarananda Bhairavan

Tantric Quest by Daniel Odier (a story of a Frenchman discovering tantra in India)

The Jewel in the Lotus by Sunyata Saraswati and Bodhi Avinasha (a practical tantra yoga book)

Tantric Awakening by Valery Brooks

Diary of a Tantric Priestess by Claire Marie Bailey with Jack Bailey

Colour Me Healing: Colourpuncture: A New Medicine of Light by Jack Allanach

In Pursuit of the Wild Prostate by rolfer-pyschologist Edward Maupin

Touching Enlightenment by Reginald A, Ray, PhD

Prostate Health in 90 days Without Drugs or Surgery by Larry Clapp

For a more comprehensive reading list, contact info@tantra.uk.com or www.tantra.uk.com.

APPENDIX V:

About Tantric Healing Massage DVD Set

In the Tantric Sex Mastery series, the *Tantric Healing Massage* DVD set will accompany this book beautifully. Both enhance each other and will create a comprehensive skill set.

TESTIMONIALS FOR THE DVDs

'These Tantric Massage Rituals will change your sex life, profound teachings and stunningly beautiful, there's no competition.'

Joseph Kramer, PhD, the 'grandfather' of erotic massage,
www.eroticmassage.com

'This is the Rolls Royce of Tantra DVDs!'

Editor, *Kindred Spirit* Magazine

'Thank you so much for the DVD. It's exactly what we need! I don't think I can fully express how grateful I am. You all gave fully of yourselves in the most generous way possible in order to share your incredible knowledge and wisdom. Our first attempts were hugely successful!! I have a lightness and optimism for our relationship that I didn't otherwise know how to find.'

S.A.

'The DVD!! Wow!!! Thank you for gifting the world with a much-needed guide to healing and transformation. It is truly inspirational. You have given me the best definition of Tantra ever ... Tantra is sacred rituals and honouring the divine in the beloved other. That has just resonated with me so deeply. As I looked at clips both upstairs and downstairs I was struck by the spirituality, sensuality, the honesty, the love, and the great sensitivity of the DVD. You, my dear sister, are a true **visionary** and wise woman. It is a testimony to who you are that there were other Tantra teachers present, saying so many wonderful things about you, the DVD. As I throw off the remaining shackles that keep me from truly being my authentic self, I look to you as teacher, mentor ... ... I give thanks to the universe for guiding me to you.'

D.W.

'Certainly the most exquisite, exciting and juicy Tantric Massage video in a long time.'

Jason – Tantra 4 Gay Men (www.tantra4gaymen.co.uk)

'This film shines with aesthetic care put into every detail. Tantra is a delicate subject, offering a sacred transmission of sex love and spirit as one unified whole. In this film, you will discover the art of Tantric Massage offered by people who live and breathe Tantra. It offers the possibility to open up and evolve in conscious love through the pleasure of touch.'

Mahasatvaa Ma Ananda Sarita (www.tantra-essence.com)

'This is a beautiful and heartful demonstration of the power of ritual in lovemaking. I highly recommend it to anyone who wants to learn to give and receive sexual pleasure with deep respect and honouring.'

Jan Day (www.janday.com)

'What a sumptuous, sensual and succulent DVD! The look, the feel, the music, the heartfelt guidance, the rituals, the real people - all of it absolutely stunning. Love it!'

Rebecca Lowrie (www.rebeccalowrie.com)

All Music was created by Craig Pruess, BAFTA award winner who has created music for *Funny Bones, Bend It Like Beckham, Bride and Prejudice, Bhaji on the Beach, The Guru, Golden Eye,* and much more. See www.heaven-on-earth-music.co.uk.

The DVD set of *Tantric Healing Massage* and the Thirteen Tantric Rituals Course is available to buy from Amazon or www.tantra.uk.com or contact info@tantra.uk.com.

APPENDIX VI:

Endorsements for This Book

Cassandra Lorius, MA, PGDip (UK)

Many women have found a neo-tantric perspective, with its female-cantered understanding of sexuality and injunction to men to devote themselves to the pleasure of their goddess, to provide a welcome change from the current male-oriented models that pervade modern media (and sex therapy) and impact on contemporary relationships. Fundamental to tantra is the notion of the body as a matrix of energy, and sex as an exchange of energy. Tantric sex is more about surrendering to the present moment, and sinking into your bodily experience, allowing your deep sexual nature to manifest and express itself freely. Orgasms arise without tension or effort and feel like waves of energy that shoot upwards throughout your body. These are called whole-body orgasms. Tantric orgasm involves the cultivation of energy in the genital area, moving it through the body, and then transmuting and directing it – whether towards pleasure, healing or spirituality.

In Hanna's accompanying DVD set, her gorgeous voice provides a confident narration to the visuals and describes how genital massage can unfold in one of three directions: healing, expanded pleasure, or expanded orgasm. The genital massage is reverential and tender and invites the viewer into an experience of sexuality that is far removed from the quick 'hand-job' that too many couples associate with genital stimulation.

Hanna's book Tantric Healing Massage for Lovers provides detailed instructions for setting the scene, and approaching your lover's body with reverence, demonstrating the mapping of the subtle anatomy of the energy body in the process of deepening pleasure and awakening sexual ecstasy. While it is hard to convey the experience, Hanna's comprehensive books describe the best ways to cultivate an attitude of honouring, as well as offering techniques so that your partner can surrender to the deep pleasure you offer during genital massage. Keep practising, until you glimpse the precious world Hanna is offering you – one that will change your experience of sex forever.'

Cassandra Lorius, MA, PGDip (Porterbrook NHS)

Sex Therapist and Author

http://www.tantricsecrets.co.uk

http://www.couplesextherapy.co.uk

(Cassandra is a sex therapist who completed a Sky Dancing UK Tantra training some fifteen years ago and has authored several best-selling books on tantra, including Tantric Sex: Making Love Last (Thorsons, 1999) and Tantric Secrets: 7 Steps to the Best Sex of Your Life (Thorsons, 2003 and now available as a Kindle eBook). She works with individuals via Skype, having trained as a sexual and relationship therapist at the Porterbrook (NHS) Clinic in Sheffield.)

Dr Tiki Adler-Raz and Zeev Adler, Israel

This is a high quality, classic book, integrative and with great depth to a practical and reference learning, enriching with a plethora of knowledge. The teachings are delivered in a comprehendible style with great sensitivity to the art of sacred sexuality. Hanna's book presents a special way the richness of the tantric nature with wonderful and detailed illustrations and pictures. These all make the guidebook easy to read, simply to understand, and inspire to carry on exploring the art of tantric massage as an exciting adventure. The book presents and offers a unique perspective, with profound and meaningful impact on our live and relationships.

Tiki Adler-Raz, PhD, and Zeev Adler
www.metaplim.co.il/tikizeev/

(Dr Tiki Adler-Raz, PhD, and Zeev Adler are partners in life and work. Tiki is an educational counsellor, Imago, CTT, Focusing and Gestalt therapist. She has an eclectic background as well as in tantra and Eastern spiritual practices. Tiki is the author of: *Tantra, When The Heart Is Ready* (2004) and *Touches* (2007). Zeev is a holistic practitioner focusing on acupuncture, traditional Thai massage, and body-related therapies. They work together as a coaching team. They lead in Israel and worldwide tantra workshops, based on body image and relationship issues.)

Deborah Anapol, PhD, Hawaii

An amazing distillation of tantric sexual knowledge! This handy guide offers a quick survey of a vast and often obscure tradition.

(Deborah Anapol, PhD, is author of *The Seven Natural Laws of Love* and *Polyamory in the 21st Century*, www.LoveWithoutLimits.com.)

Baba Dez Nichols, Arizona, USA

In this book, Hanna Katz-Jelfs has compiled a wonderful assortment Ancient and Modern Tantric information and rituals that if practiced can transform your relationships and your life.

(Baba Dez Nichols, is author of *Sacred Sexual Healing: the Shaman Method of Sex Magic*, an educator, speaker, and funder of the, International School of Temple Arts. E-mail: dez@babadez.com. Web: http://www.babadez.com, http://www.schooloftemplearts.org, Online teacher and practitioner training and educational website: http://www.templeartsproductions.com.)

Andrew Barns, Australia

One of the most comprehensive tantra books. It's a must read.

(Andrew Barns is author of *Heart of the Flower and Relationship Tantra* books. http://www.facebook.com/groups/275298602575513/ and www.awakeningwithin.org.au.)

Crystal Dawn, Arizona, USA

This beautiful book is a practical guide for bringing Tantra into your daily life and relationships. It offers clear guidance that allows you to expand your capacity for presence, pleasure, and deeper intimacy. This book opens up to a new way of living life.

(Crystal Dawn Morris, MA, is an intimacy coach, finding harmony in the flow, a certified Sky Dancing Tantra teacher at International School of Temple Arts Faculty, a certified Shamanic Breathwork facilitator, and a shamanic minister. www.tantraforawakening.com , crystal@tantraforawakening.com. 928.282.5483 Cell 928.862.0762

APPENDIX VII:

Poem

The words of the poem by Marianne Williamson, below are very important to integrate. These are the words of wisdom that Nelson Mandela chose to quote in his inaugural speech.

Our Greatest Fear:

It is our light not our darkness that most frightens us

Our deepest fear is not that we are inadequate.

Our deepest fear is that

We are powerful beyond measure.

It is our light not our darkness that most frightens us.

We ask ourselves:

Who am I to be brilliant, gorgeous, talented and fabulous?

Actually, who are you not to be?

You are a child of God.

Your playing small does not serve the world.

There's nothing enlightened about shrinking so that
other people won't feel insecure around you.

We were born to make manifest

The glory of God that is within us.

It's not just in some of us; it's in everyone.

And as we let our own light shine,

We unconsciously give other people

Permission to do the same.

As we are liberated from our own fear,

Our presence automatically liberates others.

(Marianne Williamson, from 'Return to Love')

Appendix VIII:

Tantric Terms

Amrita	Female ejaculate, nectar of the gods
Cave of brahma	Pituitary and Pineal gland in the brain
Daka	Male sacred sexual healer
Dakini	Female sacred sexual healer
Dalai Lama	Tibetan Buddhist exiled spiritual leader
Dharma	Life's purpose
Etheric	Subtle and vital body in esoteric schools
Injaculation	Inward ejaculation
Ketchari mudra	Position of the tongue inside the mouth towards the back of the throat
Kum ney	Tibetan healing yoga practices
Kundalini	Sexual or orgasmic energy, raw sexual energy, life force energy
Lingam	Penis
Maithuna	Ultimate tantric sacred union
Manas	Mind

Mandala	Sacred geometrical shape
Meridians	Major energy pathways in the body
Mukti	Royal liberation Mantra
Nadis	Energy pathways in the body
Namaste	An honouring gesture meaning, 'I Salute the divinity within you.'
Nidra	A form of yoga practiced during deep relaxation
Niyasa	Honoring gesture ritual
NO	Nitric oxide
Ojas	Life/love juices
Rudra veena	Rare tantric musical instrument, similar to a sitar with two goads
Sadhana	Daily practice
Sacred gate	G-Spot
Sacred spot	G-Spot
Sacred union	Sexual intercourse
Shiva	God, man, masculinity
Shakti	Goddess, woman, femininity
So ham	'I am that I am', compassion mantra, graceful swan
Tatva	Rites, rituals
Tattva	Elements, aspects of reality
Turia	Deep state of sleep reaching a state of bliss
Vajra Penis	

Vajrayana	The Buddhist tantric path, thunder-bolt lightening path
Yoni	Vagina, vulva, sacred place, tomb

ABOUT THE AUTHOR

Hanna Katz-Jelfs was born in Givaataym, Israel and has been living in the UK since 1981. Her father's surname is Katz, which is an abbreviation of the words *kohen* meaning 'priest', and *tzedek* meaning 'justice'. 'Katz' means high-justice priest; this is Hanna's heritage and family origins. Jelfs is Hanna's English husband's surname. Her spiritual name is Maha Shakti Kali Ma.

Hanna's heritage is Kabbalist. Her late father was from Satmare in Hungary, now part of Romania. He survived the holocaust and Auschwitz, and the Buddhist teachings of karma helped him through the horrors of memories and nightmares. Hanna's mother was born in France and was also a survivor of the Holocaust; she was saved by nuns after the Vichy police killed her father and sister. Hanna's family expected a healer. She was born with a perfect birthmark on her forehead, at the inner guru, the fourth eye place, and was branded the Indian of the family. The spiritual name, Maha Kali is given to females born with insights and the birth mark on the third or fourth eye.

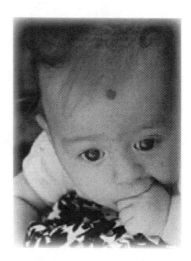

Image 56: Hanna Maha Kali

By the age of two, Hanna's favourite game was pretending to be the Buddha. She had past-life memories throughout her childhood and a recurring dream that she took off her human 'suit' and mask and the light shone. Much later she learned that this is a Kabbalistic teaching – that we are of the light. At age ten Hanna had a premonition and saw the death of a newly wedded member of the family. When this came true, she realized her visions were both a gift and a curse.

At thirteen Hanna had a sexual initiation and was opened to the secret powers of the life force energies surging through her body. By fourteen she mastered the ability, without touch, to bring orgasms rushing through the whole body, illuminating and exploding at each chakra. This inspired her exploration for a new kind of intimacy. Decades later she learnt these were the practices and effects of the cobra breath.

Owing to her spiritual beliefs, Hanna knew that she could not meet the demands of her country to serve in the Israeli army, and at seventeen, she left behind her family and friends to start a new life in the UK.

After two failed pregnancies and marriages, she returned in 1996 to Israel with her daughter. Hanna realized that she no longer belonged there, but rather she belonged nowhere … and everywhere. This was a liberating revelation. They moved back to the UK.

After a period of time on a celibate tantric spiritual path practicing Tai Chi, yoga, and meditations, Hanna was ready to engage in the world of relationships. She met her husband Martin Jelfs. As they were both practicing and working with tantra prior to meeting, it was a conscious relationship and remains so to this day.

Hanna spent more than thirty-five years studying many spiritual teachings and traditional Eastern methods of spirituality, healing, and intimacy. She was a degree lecturer, a qualified architect, and a psychodynamic therapist specializing in relationships and psychosexual therapies.

In 1998 Hanna and Martin established a tantra school in the UK called Transcendence. They have been teaching together: tantra for couples, singles, *tantra kriya* yoga (the cosmic cobra breath initiations), and tantric healing massage, as well as bringing international teachers to enhance teachings on tantra and sacred sexuality.

Hanna's DVDs have been acknowledged by peers as one of the best on tantric intimacy. See DVD testimonials in appendix V. These are said to be the 'Rolls Royce of the Tantra DVDs'.

Hanna now helps people create relationships that are more intimate and fulfilling. She only works with people who are ready to propel their relationships to a whole new dimension. Her passion is the yoga of relationships, healing, and the art of honouring sacred sexuality. Hanna's mission is to leave people feeling elated, blissful, and orgasmic with life!